Other Books in the Historic Restaurants Series™

Arizona's Historic Restaurants and Their Recipes
by Karen Surina Mulford

Florida's Historic Restaurants and Their Recipes
by Dawn O'Brien and Becky Roper Matkov

Georgia's Historic Restaurants and Their Recipes
by Dawn O'Brien and Jean Spaugh

Maryland's Historic Restaurants and Their Recipes
by Dawn O'Brien and Rebecca Schenck

North Carolina's Historic Restaurants and Their Recipes
by Dawn O'Brien

Pennsylvania's Historic Restaurants and Their Recipes
by Dawn O'Brien and Claire Walter

South Carolina's Historic Restaurants and Their Recipes
by Dawn O'Brien and Karen Mulford

Virginia's Historic Restaurants and Their Recipes
by Dawn O'Brien

Alabama's Historic Restaurants
and Their Recipes

Alabama's Historic Restaurants and Their Recipes

by Gay N. Martin

For Tracie —
Wishing you all
that's good —
Gay Martin
Merry Christmas
1999

John F. Blair, Publisher
Winston-Salem, North Carolina

DESIGN BY DEBRA LONG HAMPTON
MAP BY THE ROBERTS GROUP
PHOTOGRAPHS BY CARLTON AND GAY MARTIN EXCEPT WHERE NOTED.
PHOTOGRAPH ON FRONT COVER BY STOCKER PHOTOGRAPHY, FAIRHOPE, ALABAMA
PHOTOGRAPH ON BACK COVER BY LLOYD ANDREWS, STUDIO ONE, ANNISTON, ALABAMA
PRINTED AND BOUND BY R. R. DONNELLEY & SONS

Library of Congress Cataloging-in-Publication Data
Martin, Gay N.
Alabama's historic restaurants and their recipes / by Gay N. Martin.
        p.   cm.   -- (Historic restaurants series)
                Includes index.
        ISBN 0-89587-220-X (alk. paper)
    1. Cookery, American--Southern style.   2. Cookery--Alabama.
3. Restaurants--Alabama--Gudiebooks.   4. Historic buildings--Alabama   I. Title   II. Series.
            TX715.2.S68M325   1998
        614.59761--dc21   98-38055

Preface

*W*hile researching this book, I discovered that Alabama's diverse geography offers a feast for all, whether the entree of choice is mountain climbing or beachcombing. The state's natural beauty ranges from rugged mountain peaks in the north to sugary sand beaches on the Gulf of Mexico.

From mountains to shore, from cotton-bordered hamlets to cityscapes, this book profiles fifty restaurants and includes two or three tempting, kitchen-tested recipes from each. The featured restaurants range from rustic and simple to cosmopolitan and posh.

All are housed in buildings with a past. The books in this series feature structures at least fifty years old. Many are listed on the National Register of Historic Places and have played pivotal roles in the state's history. Others lack such credentials but rank as landmark buildings in their respective communities. Across Alabama, I dined in rustic log cabins, white-columned mansions, carriageways, grand Victorian homes, and former banks, drugstores, gas stations, schoolhouses, department stores, and warehouses.

True, the state's food heritage centers on traditional fare like fried chicken, mashed potatoes, homemade biscuits, salt-cured country ham, cornbread, and vegetables. Still, from fried catfish and hickory-smoked barbecue to rack of lamb and chicken cordon bleu, I found a varied menu while eating my way through Alabama.

I visited chefs who wore crisp white jackets, designer outfits, and aprons both fancy and mundane. Many people I interviewed grew up cooking. Some polished their talents in cooking schools in Paris, Hyde Park, New England, and California. Others did so at home under the tutelage of a gifted mother or grandmother. Many chefs took time from their hectic schedules to explain techniques and show me the kitchen studios where they create their masterpieces of culinary art. At Troup House Restaurant in Selma's St. James Hotel, Chef Barnett Blair even produced a couple of vanilla beans from his toolbox for a recipe I needed to try.

Birmingham and the surrounding area brim with exceptional restaurants. In the historic Five Points South area, one can enjoy an outdoor lunch at Cobb Lane Restaurant or dinner at Highlands Bar & Grill, where the Southern cuisine whispers of Provence. Nearby, downhome country cooking beckons at The Irondale Cafe, the inspiration for Fannie Flagg's *Fried Green Tomatoes at the Whistle-Stop Cafe*.

In Montgomery, the options range from Asian cuisine at Lek's Railroad Thai at Union Station to enlightened Southern fare served in a plantation setting at Panache at Rose Hill.

In charming Mobile, I savored seafood at some of the city's best restaurants. Throughout the Port City and along Alabama's gulf coast, many local fish markets will pack fresh seafood in ice for travelers, and I always take home a cooler of shrimp, jumbo lump crabmeat, and snapper.

Other cities like Tuscaloosa and Dothan boast brewpubs housed in historic buildings. In addition to making their own beers on the premises and providing sports-bar fare, some of these reincarnated structures house white-tablecloth restaurants.

In the course of my travels, I sampled palate-pleasing continental offerings at Tuscaloosa's Mezzanine and filled my plate at The Gift Horse in Foley, where the daily banquets feature everything from Jellied Bing Cherries and Nut Salad to White Chocolate Cake.

Writing this book often sent me from the keyboard to the cutting board—from splicing paragraphs to dicing potatoes. During past books, my husband commented that our quality of life suffered. My kitchen, which normally produces wonderful meals, would shut down during the last hectic weeks before my deadline. But instead of picking up fast food during the countdown days, my coverage of Alabama's historic restaurants allowed me to prepare and savor Justine's Courtyard & Carriageway's Crab Cakes, LOUISIANA The Restaurant's Chicken Lafayette, GainesRidge's Snapper Special, and The Bright Star's Tenderloin of Beef Greek-Style. Each day's lunch and dinner became part of my writing assignment. Many recipes in this book have already made their way to luncheons, dinner parties, and church suppers.

If reading this book makes you hungry, then strike out for one of Alabama's historic restaurants. Be sure to call ahead, because hours and menus change. If a visit is not feasible, then step into your own kitchen and whip up one of the recipes included here. Whether your specialty is spreading the sandwich mixture carefully to the edges of the bread, or whether you routinely reduce sauces and plunge protesting lobsters into boiling water, you'll find some recipes in this book to make your own. So get started on your Alabama dining adventure — and enjoy a heaping helping of hospitality and history.

Acknowledgments

$\mathcal{M}$any wonderful people helped me with this book, and like an Oscar recipient acknowledging her talented crew, I hope I don't leave anyone out.

First, I want to thank all the chefs and restaurateurs who provided recipes and shared their time and culinary talents.

The Alabama Bureau of Tourism and Travel provided invaluable assistance and material. Throughout the state, many convention and visitor bureaus and chambers of commerce assisted in my search for historic restaurants. I especially want to thank Ami Simpson, Cameron Reeder, Georgia Carter Turner, Patty Tucker, Pam Swanner, Squee Bailey, Lee Sentell, Robin McClellan, Jean Ann Oglesby, Mary Katherine Zarzaur, Lou Anne Dulaney, Susan Eller, Frances Tucker, Heather Rickles, Hester Cope, Debbie Wilson, Lisa O. Socha, Kelly Sauer, Lin Graham, Laurie S. Cothran, Pat Dakin, Martha Hollis, Mary Alice Patterson, Toni Johnson-Purry, Kay Carroll, Marilyn Townsend, and Carol Parham.

An enormous thank-you goes to the friends who helped me test and taste the recipes in this book. I know they're friends, because who else would spend a day making three Thai dishes plus a cheesecake and then bring them all over for a surprise supper? Or take a Saturday driving tour all over Huntsville in search of pickled ginger? Or defy a snowstorm to transport a home-baked chocolate cake from Birmingham?

So the following friends should consider themselves hugged: Jeri and Malcolm Windrow, Gayle and Ira Crawford, Terri and Ed Miholits, Betty Sue Towers, Annilee Brumlik, Nancy Jo Hardy, Joan and Neal Broerman, Joyce White, Jennifer Teall, Kathleen and Jack Gocek, Angie, Mike, Paul, and Steven Brindley, Madeleine Appleton, Billiejean Bruce, Laura Casey, Faye Copous, Ruth Gregory, Joyce Henderson, Helen Haynie, Tricia Hoerth, Bettye Jolley, Iva Jo Maddux, Darlene Kellison, Anna McChesney, Malinda Karr, Martha Lacy, Christine Ladshaw, Carolyn Mason, Jill Mitchem, Evelyne Morris, Joyce O'Brien, Reba Smith, Winifred Wells, Barbara Williamson, Karen Gipson, Sandy Barkley, and Mary Kay Remich.

Special thanks for photo assistance goes to Mary Katherine Zarzaur, Jean Ann Oglesby, Heather Rickles, Debbie Deese, Barbara Duke, Shirley Sandy, and John Chumley. Others who contributed to this project include Frances Roberts, Frank Bauer, Robin Cooper, Betty and Jack Powell, Wilda Eddy, and Cindy Maddux.

Also, I'd like to acknowledge the following persons for their contributions: Denise Marcil (my agent), Sue Clark, Steve Kirk, Karen Surina Mulford, Tom Scott, Carolyn Bennett, Ann Moon Rabb, Rick Daidone, Bob Kelley, David Monroe, Michael Pierce, Nancy Gross, John Krontiras, Wanda Walker, Dr. Eugene Mangieri, Chad McCowan, Jeanne Hodgins, Carolyn and Felix Vereen, Trisha Griess, and the two Lynns. I'm also grateful to family members Lisa and Jack Hancock for their culinary assistance. And an enormous thank-you goes to my family and especially to Carlton Martin — my husband and best friend.

Dedication

This book is for my favorite dentist, Carlton Martin.

Contents

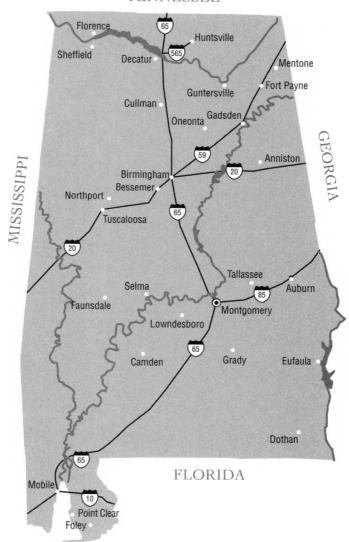

TENNESSEE

Florence
Sheffield
Decatur
Huntsville
Mentone
Fort Payne
Guntersville
Cullman
Oneonta
Gadsden
Anniston
Birmingham
Bessemer
Northport
Tuscaloosa
Selma
Tallassee
Auburn
Faunsdale
Montgomery
Lowndesboro
Camden
Grady
Eufaula
Dothan
Mobile
Point Clear
Foley

MISSISSIPPI

GEORGIA

FLORIDA

Alabama

The Victoria

1604 Quintard Avenue
ANNISTON

$\mathcal{N}$ever your typical town, Anniston chose William Shakespeare as its citizen of the year in 1984 — before the Alabama Shakespeare Festival left its birthplace here and moved to Montgomery.

Founded in 1872 by the Noble and Tyler families, "Annie's Town" (named for Annie Scott Tyler) did not evolve in haphazard fashion. For this self-styled "Model City of the South," community planners plotted business, industrial, and residential sections before selling construction sites. Then stonemasons came from England to build schools and churches, such as the stately Church of St. Michael.

On a hill along tree-lined Quintard Avenue in Anniston's Tyler Hill Historic District stands The Victoria. A burgundy awning covers the walkway to the turreted three-story structure, painted vanilla with white trim.

Early Anniston Land Company partner, Confederate veteran, and two-time gubernatorial candidate John McKleroy built the grand Victorian home in 1888. Later, the Wilson family lived here, then the Kirby family. The main house's three lovely upstairs suites, decorated in period antiques, are named for these former owners.

Listed on the National Register of Historical Places in 1984 and now owned by Betty and Earlon McWhorter, The Victoria continues to spellbind visitors with its Queen Anne charm. Earlon McWhorter, the contractor for the preservation project, and architect Julian Jenkins transformed the home into a country inn. A guesthouse and an attractive addition with individually decorated rooms provide more accommodations.

Following the covered walkway that wraps around the inn's courtyard and pool, I made my way to the main house's dining room — actually two connecting rooms with charming Victorian furnishings. Open to the public for dinner, the restaurant has a menu that changes seasonally but always offers steaks and fresh seafood, including the celebrated Jumbo Lump Crab Cakes.

For an appetizer, I chose Fried Green Tomatoes with Lime Crème Fraîche and tasso ham, although the chef's daily soup creation sounded tempting. Because I never turn down crab cakes, choosing an entree was easy for me. Sautéed and served with wild rice pilaf, my entree lived up to its reputation, bits of red and gold pepper adding both flavor and visual appeal to the chef's interpretation. The menu might feature Tenderloin of Beef with Parmesan cheese, fresh herbs, and garlic or Baked Atlantic Salmon.

The Victoria offers a wide selection of wines. The ever-popular desserts include Bourbon Pecan Pie and homemade Cheesecake topped with seasonal fruit or perhaps drizzled with chocolate.

And "The Vic" (as the locals call it) promises another treat. Just a stroll away, an old carriage house on the grounds contains an art gallery known as Wren's Nest, which showcases original works and limited-edition prints by noted wildlife artist Larry K. Martin.

The Victoria's Jumbo Lump Crab Cakes

1 pound jumbo lump
  crabmeat
2 cups breadcrumbs
½ cup mayonnaise
1 bunch green onions,
  chopped

½ red bell pepper, chopped
½ gold bell pepper, chopped
salt and pepper to taste
juice of ½ lemon
Wine Butter Sauce (recipe
  below)

Place crabmeat and breadcrumbs in a bowl. When breadcrumbs are moist, add remaining ingredients except for Wine Butter Sauce. Shape into four 5-ounce patties. Sauté in butter until golden brown, turning once. Remove from pan and set aside. Serve with Wine Butter Sauce. Yields 4 crab cakes.

Wine Butter Sauce

1 tablespoon butter
2 tablespoons shallots, diced
  fine
¼ cup white wine

⅓ cup heavy cream
½ cup unsalted butter
juice of ½ lemon
salt and pepper to taste

Melt butter in a sauté pan. Add shallots and lightly sauté until translucent. Deglaze with white wine and reduce. Add cream and continue to reduce. When cream thickens, reduce heat and whisk in unsalted butter. Adjust seasoning with lemon and salt and pepper.

The Victoria's Baked Atlantic Salmon

2 6- to 7-ounce salmon
   fillets, deboned
½ cup white wine
2 shallots, minced

1 tablespoon margarine
salt and pepper
1 lemon, sliced

Place salmon in 400-degree oven for 8 to 10 minutes. Remove from pan. Deglaze with white wine. Add shallots. Add margarine and stir until melted. Add salt and pepper to taste and garnish with lemon. Serves 2.

The Victoria's Fennel Mashed Potatoes

2½ pounds red-skinned
   potatoes
1 bulb fennel
½ cup sour cream

¼ cup butter
¼ cup heavy cream
salt and pepper

Wash and peel potatoes. Cover with water and add fennel. Boil until done, then strain. Mash with fork, then fold in sour cream and butter. Adjust consistency with cream. Add salt and pepper to taste. Serves 8.

The Olde Warehouse

315 South Second Street
GADSDEN

"Sure, I could give you my Squash Casserole recipe, but then I'd have to kill you," Chef Mike Bradford jested as we sat at a table in The Olde Warehouse.

The restaurant's lunch crowd comes here for the honest country flavors of the daily vegetable-plate specials. "We cut the corn off the cob," Bradford said. "We peel the potatoes. Everything is fresh." In season, Fried Green Tomatoes often make the menu.

The restaurant serves six hundred persons a day, so it's best to arrive early for lunch, before the daily quota of fresh vegetables dwindles. Of course, you can also order from the menu, which features such favorites as Seafood Gumbo and Chicken Noodle Soup, made fresh daily, along with salads, burgers, sandwiches, and steaks.

After my server reeled off a list that included Butter Beans, Fried Okra, and Mashed Potatoes with Gravy, I started to order: "I'll take the Squash and —"

"You only have to choose a meat," she said, "And today, we have Grilled Chicken Breast, Chicken and Dumplings, Chicken Pot Pie, Meatloaf, and Fried Chicken Livers. You get *all* the vegetables."

And I certainly did — plus Cornbread and Peach Cobbler.

The party atmosphere heats up with live music nightly. Dinners run to steaks and seafood. The chef's flavorful Seared Rib-Eye with Mushrooms and Onions ranks high on the list of Olde Warehouse favorites. Prime Rib is available on Friday and Saturday evenings.

The Oyster Bar's "S.O.B. nights" draw a crowd, too. "Be sure and translate that," said Cathey Mackey, who owns the restaurant with her husband, Kenneth. "S.O.B. stands for shrimp, oysters, and a pitcher of beer. We offer these at reduced prices on Tuesday evenings."

Constructed in the early 1900s as a storage facility for cotton that arrived by rail, the building was later reincarnated as a lounge. The Olde Warehouse became a restaurant about a decade ago. The restored structure has accents of barn red and hunter green and features a cen-

Lunch
11:00 A.M. until 2:00 P.M.
Monday through Friday

Dinner
5:00 P.M. until 10:00 P.M.
Monday through Thursday
5:00 P.M. until 11:00 P.M.
Friday and Saturday

For reservations (recommended for groups at lunch and for dinner), call (256) 547-5548.

trally placed bar. A cranny over the front entrance houses an antique organ. Nearby, an elevated sleigh glows with Christmas lights throughout the year.

Refueled by a hearty lunch, I sallied forth to take in a photography exhibit at downtown Gadsden's Center for Cultural Arts.

The Olde Warehouse's Squash Casserole

7 medium crookneck squash,
  sliced
1 medium onion, chopped
½ bell pepper, diced
2 eggs, beaten

2 cups cracker crumbs
½ pound Velveeta cheese,
  cubed
½ cup milk
salt, pepper, and sugar to
  taste

Cook squash in boiling water until tender; drain and set aside. Sauté onion and bell pepper, then combine with squash and all remaining ingredients except ½ cup of the cracker crumbs. Place in a casserole dish or baking pan and sprinkle with reserved cracker crumbs. Bake at 350 degrees for 30 minutes. Serves 8.

The Olde Warehouse's Seared Rib-Eye with Mushrooms and Onions

2½ teaspoons Lawry's
  seasoning
1½ teaspoons cumin
½ teaspoon garlic, minced
½ teaspoon black pepper

2 10-ounce rib-eye steaks
1 mild onion, sliced
2 shiitake mushrooms, sliced
1 tablespoon butter

Rub spices into steaks. Cook on a flat grill until done. Sauté onion and mushrooms in butter, place on steaks and serve. Serves 2.

Sweetbriar Restaurant

1000 Forrest Avenue
GADSDEN

*O*fficially called Nancy's Grosseries, Inc., at Sweetbriar, this restaurant occupies a lovely home that dates to 1905. Nancy and Bob Gross purchased Sweetbriar because it seemed the perfect setting to showcase Nancy's creative cuisine.

Dr. Arthur William Ralls, whose portrait hangs in a front dining room, built the home but soon sold it to finance the construction of a local hospital. The structure then served as an office for Dr. Charles Lloyd Lawson and later housed an outdoor supply company for his son, Larry.

11:00 A.M. until 3:00 P.M.
Sunday through Wednesday

11:00 A.M. until 9:00 P.M.
Thursday through Saturday

Alcohol is not served. For reservations (requested), call (256) 546-0900.

In 1990, Martha Holcomb bought the property, renovated the home, and named it Sweetbriar. In this charming setting, she and her design staff created Miss Martha's Originals, a line of collectible figurines.

Then along came Nancy, who immediately recognized Sweetbriar's potential as a restaurant. She knew it would be especially appealing thanks to Miss Martha's state-of-the-art commercial kitchen. "On opening day," Nancy said, "we dedicated the kitchen to my mother and father." Elegantly restored and beautifully decorated with antique sideboards and custom-made marble-topped tables on pedestals, Sweetbriar exudes a comfortable Victorian ambiance.

Nancy, who previously operated a restaurant and catering business in nearby Attalla, describes her cuisine as a "unique blending of culinary delights and healthful foods." She has an extensive background in nutrition as a licensed, registered dietitian and champions healthy eating. Better yet, her dishes ooze with flavor without being slathered in butter. She enjoys "southernizing traditional recipes," as she puts it. Nancy says that her New England background and her experience living in the South for the past two decades make for an interesting blending of styles.

The inspiration for her Lemon Chicken Orzo Soup came from visits to a Greek deli in Andover, Massachusetts, where Nancy often picked up comfort food during her mother's illness. And Nancy puts her own spin on New Orleans's famous Muffaletta, a hero-type sandwich on French bread with meat, provolone cheese, and an olive salad mixture. Recently, she used her culinary expertise to create Fresh Tomato Mango

Slaw, a dish that took first-place honors at a local festival, the Tomato Jubilee.

Daily specials include such dishes as Pork Tenderloin and Lemon Pepper Chicken and Pasta. A signature dish is the Southern Comfort Plate, which features Baked Chicken Pulley Bone (a special cut using the wishbone section of the chicken breast, which Nancy calls "the medallion of the chicken") and vegetables.

Among the tempting items on Sweetbriar's dessert tray, the Blonde Brownie proves a perennial favorite.

Although Sweetbriar does not serve alcohol, its BYOW policy permits brown-bagging, so patrons who wish to enjoy wine with dinner may bring their own.

Sweetbriar Restaurant's Lemon Chicken Orzo Soup

1½ cups orzo
2 tablespoons chicken soup
  base
2 quarts water

2 cups chicken, cooked and
  shredded
¼ cup fresh lemon juice
2 cans cream of chicken soup
salt and pepper

Cook orzo according to package directions, drain, and rinse. Mix chicken soup base in 2 quarts water. Add chicken and lemon juice. Fold in orzo. Just before serving, add cream of chicken soup. Heat through, but do not let mixture boil. Season to taste.

Yields approximately 3 quarts.

Note: Cream of chicken soup may be replaced by egg whites (about 3). Have soup softly boiling. Wire-whip egg whites until frothy, then fold into soup. Serve immediately.

Sweetbriar Restaurant's Baked Chicken Pulley Bone

6 whole boneless chicken
   breasts
1 cup nonfat plain yogurt
½ cup cashews, chopped fine
4 ounces Waverly crackers,
   crushed fine

1½ cups biscuit mix
2 teaspoons Cajun seasoning
2 teaspoons Old Bay
   seasoning
1½ teaspoons paprika
1 teaspoon salt

Trim each chicken breast to yield pulley bone portion (or medallion). Reserve remainder of chicken for another use. Coat chicken pieces in yogurt. Mix remaining ingredients in a shallow bowl. Dredge chicken in breading mix and place several inches apart in a baking pan. Spray tops of chicken pieces with Pam. Bake in a preheated 400-degree oven about 45 minutes or until done. Serves 6.

Sweetbriar Restaurant's Blonde Brownies

⅓ cup butter, melted
1 cup light brown sugar
1 egg
1 teaspoon vanilla
1 cup all-purpose flour
½ cup pecans, chopped

½ cup milk chocolate chips
½ cup butterscotch chips
½ cup Heath Toffee Crunch
   (bits of brittle)
vanilla ice cream
caramel syrup

Preheat oven to 350 degrees. Grease an 8- by 8-inch pan. Mix butter and brown sugar. Add egg, vanilla, and flour. Fold in nuts. Spread dough in pan and sprinkle chips and brittle on top. Bake at 350 degrees for 15 to 25 minutes. Warm prior to serving. Serve with vanilla ice cream and drizzle with caramel syrup. Yields 16 brownies.

Little River Cafe

Fischer Crossroads on Lookout Mountain Parkway
(DeSoto Parkway)
FORT PAYNE

$\mathcal{L}$ ittle River Cafe is located five minutes from downtown Fort Payne in tiny Fischer. The history of this community reads like a Hollywood tale—a German love story with a Romeo-and-Juliet flavor. Thankfully, Fischer's version ends happily.

In the early 1850s, Gustavus Fischer came to America from the Bavarian Alps. His mission: to find his true love, Caroline Sutterlin, whose family had whisked her away from Hulgelheim, Germany, and from Gus himself, allegedly the local Don Juan.

11:00 A.M. until 8:30 P.M.
Monday through Thursday

11:00 A.M. until 9:30 P.M.
Friday and Saturday

No alcoholic beverages are served. No reservations are taken. For information, call (256) 997-0707.

After a dedicated search that lasted several years, Gus traced Caroline to northern Georgia. By that time, Caroline's parents saw their daughter's pursuer in a new light—as a man with a strong sense of purpose—and permitted him to carry Caroline over the threshold.

After the wedding, the couple moved to an area on Lookout Mountain. Gus had discovered it during his search and had vowed to settle there once he found Caroline. On a homestead of 640 acres, he made a living by farming and operating a sawmill, a shingle mill, and a grist-mill. Completely embracing his adopted homeland, he fought for the Confederacy during the Civil War.

Each of the couple's six children received forty acres and a house— built from Gus's own timber and processed at his sawmill. The construction of a home for his grandson Luke, the son of Henry Fischer, marked the conclusion of Gus's projects. This modest structure with porch columns cut from cedar trees now houses Little River Cafe.

Those same cedar trees were planted in the front yard by Caroline and Gus many years ago. When the trees started to decay, the Goggans family—a later owner—cut them for use as columns for their cafe. While renovating the structure, they stripped away plasterboard walls to expose the original lumber from Gus Fischer's sawmill. A fine rock chimney discovered during the process now serves as a focal point of the eatery.

Rustic and unique, the cafe's interior features cozy nooks and crannies decorated with equestrian items and John Wayne memorabilia.

Two columns contain tucked-away bookcases filled with novels like *The Adventures of Huckleberry Finn* and assorted paperbacks. Vintage ladies' hats and purses hang in a back corner near the bandstand, which is used on weekends for live entertainment. "Pickin' and Grinnin'" is featured on Friday and Saturday nights.

On the crisp fall day when I visited, the Saturday Chili Special sounded tempting. The cafe's tasty version starts with a base of marinara sauce.

The daily lunch specials vary but always include a meat with three vegetables and a dessert.

"Half the food I serve is stuff I like to eat," said Donny Baldwin, one of the owners of this family-run business. Donny strives for a menu that appeals to kids — or, perhaps more accurately, to the kid in everyone. Among the favorites are Quesadillas and Cheesy Chili Chicken Salad with homemade Mexicali Dressing.

Little River Cafe's Mexicali Dressing

1 cup ketchup
⅔ cup mayonnaise
1 teaspoon chili powder

½ teaspoon garlic powder
1 teaspoon Worcestershire
sauce

Combine all ingredients. Serve as a dipping sauce or salad dressing. Yields 2 cups.

Little River Cafe's Apple Cinnamon Crunch

16-ounce can apples
16-ounce box yellow cake
mix

½ cup margarine, melted
½ teaspoon cinnamon

Place apples in a baking dish or pan. Cover with cake mix, drizzle with margarine, then sprinkle with cinnamon. Bake at 350 degrees for 15 to 20 minutes or until golden brown. Serves 8.

*16-ounce can sliced peaches,
 undrained*
½ cup sugar
¼ cup margarine
1½ teaspoons cinnamon

pinch of salt
2 tablespoons shortening
1 cup flour
several tablespoons ice water

Combine peaches, sugar, margarine, cinnamon, and salt in a saucepan. Bring mixture to a boil, remove from heat, and pour into a 2-quart baking dish. Work shortening into flour, adding ice water as needed to make soft dough. Roll out dough to size of baking dish and cover peach mixture. If desired, brush with melted margarine and sprinkle with sugar. Bake at 400 degrees for 25 minutes or until crust browns. Serves 6.

Mountain Inn Restaurant

DeSoto State Park Lodge
13883 DeKalb County Road 89
FORT PAYNE

Showcasing spectacular vistas, Alabama's state parks offer both beauty and recreational options. DeSoto State Park, one of the oldest, is situated in the state's northeastern corner and boasts a lodge of hand-hewn native stone. The lodge was completed in 1935 by members of the Civilian Conservation Corps (CCC) under the National Park Service's direction. Using an old quarry north of the campground, CCC stonemasons fashioned giant abstract jigsaw puzzles from blocks of sandstone interspersed with quartzite and granite. Their expert workmanship can also be seen in other buildings dotting the grounds.

Breakfast
7:00 A.M. until 10:00 A.M.

Lunch
11:30 A.M. until 3:00 P.M.

Lunch Buffet
11:30 A.M. until 3:00 P.M.
Sunday

Dinner
5:00 P.M. until 8:00 P.M.
Sunday through Thursday

5:00 P.M. until 9:00 P.M.
Friday and Saturday

No alcoholic beverages are served.
For reservations, call (256) 845-5380
or (800) 568-8840.

Food was served in the lodge during the thirties and forties. Later, as a community center, it became the setting for dances and dinners. An A-frame glass enclosure now camouflages the original entrance, but stepping inside, you can fully appreciate the fine rock structure. Today, it houses a large restaurant with three dining rooms.

To fortify ourselves for a day of discovery in this secluded mountaintop getaway, my husband and I decided to forgo our usual fruit and cereal and indulge in one of the lodge's substantial Southern breakfasts. In choosing a table, we considered the Canyon Room, where original stained-glass windows flank a large fireplace. The nip in the air made this room with its glowing logs tempting, but the adjacent stone porch won us over, thanks to its view of the spectacular fall foliage. The restaurant offers a country breakfast buffet with Eggs, Sausage, Bacon, Grits, Hash Browns, Biscuits, and Gravy.

Favorite lunch items include the Crown Chicken Salad Platter and Reuben and Executive Club Sandwiches. For dinner, the Crispy Catfish is popular. It features two whole pond-raised catfish served with Hush Puppies, Slaw, and your choice of potato.

Lodge manager Bela Novak shared his recipes for Cabbage and Potato Soup, Beef Stroganoff, and a light, layered dessert named in honor of Patty Tucker, an avid promoter of DeSoto State Park and other DeKalb County attractions.

To enjoy the area's magnificent terrain, visitors can book a room, chalet, or cabin. Recreational activities include rafting, canoeing, and hiking along miles of trails bordered in summer by Queen Anne's lace, honeysuckle, and black-eyed Susans. The park extends about forty miles along Little River, a unique waterway whose complete course runs atop a mountain. Spectacular De Soto Falls is nearby. The property's southern section features views of Little River Canyon, the largest and one of the deepest gorges east of the Mississippi River.

With five thousand acres of breathtaking beauty to explore, it's no wonder that weekend hikers favor the hearty meals served by Novak and his staff.

Mountain Inn Restaurant's Cabbage and Potato Soup

3 cups chicken broth
2 cups shredded cabbage
2 medium potatoes, peeled
   and diced
2 tablespoons butter
1 cup leeks, chopped
3 tablespoons flour

3 cups milk
2 teaspoons Dijon mustard
1 teaspoon Worcestershire
   sauce
½ teaspoon caraway seeds
few drops Tabasco sauce
salt and pepper to taste

Heat chicken broth and add cabbage and potatoes. Add butter and leeks and cook until vegetables are tender. Add flour and cook 3 minutes. Add remaining ingredients and cook 10 to 15 minutes. Yields about 3½ pints.

Mountain Inn Restaurant's Beef Stroganoff

1 pound beef tips
2 tablespoons vegetable oil
½ cup margarine
2 tablespoons flour
1 large onion, chopped
pinch of garlic powder
2 cups chicken broth
2 drops Tabasco sauce

1 teaspoon prepared mustard
1 teaspoon beef base
   (commercial)
1 can cream of mushroom
   soup
2 tablespoons cooking sherry
1 cup sour cream
egg noodles

Brown beef tips in vegetable oil; set aside. Melt margarine, then stir in flour. Brown. Add chopped onions and cook 5 minutes. Add remaining ingredients except sherry and sour cream and cook slowly for 30 minutes, stirring occasionally. Just before serving, stir in sherry and sour cream. Serve over egg noodles. Serves 4.

Mountain Inn Restaurant's Patty's Sunrise

½ cup nuts, chopped fine
1 cup flour
½ cup margarine, softened
16-ounce container Cool
   Whip, thawed

8-ounce package cream
   cheese, softened
1 cup powdered sugar
8-serving package instant
   lemon pudding
3 cups milk

Toss nuts with flour and work in margarine until well blended. Press in bottom of a 9- by 12-inch pan. Bake at 350 degrees for 20 minutes. Cool. Beat half of Cool Whip with cream cheese and powdered sugar until smooth and creamy. Spread over crust. Combine pudding mix with milk and spread over cream cheese mixture. Top with remaining Cool Whip. If desired, sprinkle with additional nuts and with ½ teaspoon grated lemon rind for added zest. Refrigerate for 2 hours or until set. Serves 12.

Cragsmere Manna

17871 DeKalb County Road 89
MENTONE

$\mathcal{A}$bout three miles from the charming village of Mentone (named after a French resort town on the Riviera) stands Cragsmere Manna, a restaurant housed in one of Lookout Mountain's oldest structures.

The Cragsmere tradition started in 1898, when Ned Jackson, a former slave from Virginia, and his wife, Margrette, acquired this property and its log cabin from W. N. Howell. A popular setting for Sunday picnics, the Jackson place soon gained a reputation for good food and hospitality.

Following the Jacksons' residence, a 1927 real-estate venture resulted in the property's conversion to the Cragsmer Club. (The final *e* was added to the spelling later.) The owners enlarged the original cabin for use as a clubhouse and lodging facility. Guests traveled from New Orleans, Montgomery, Birmingham, and elsewhere to enjoy the invigorating mountain air, horseback riding, fishing, golf, tennis, and hiking. Such activities made them work up hearty appetites for the club's home-cooked meals, served family-style.

The Gifford family occupied the home from 1931 to 1937, after which the Ferrells, who had managed nearby Mentone Springs Hotel during the 1920s, purchased the property. Nina Ferrell cooked memorable meals — most notably, her chicken-and-biscuit breakfasts — on a wood-burning stove.

Charmed by the place's ambiance, Ronnie and Bonnie Barnett bought the property in 1988. Today, they continue the Cragsmere tradition with what they call a "country gourmet" restaurant.

Each of Cragsmere's six dining areas offers its own brand of charm. Diners can see the original cabin's hand-hewn log walls in the Heritage Dining Room. The back porch — another favorite — makes a great place for summertime sunset watching.

On the day we visited, my husband and I heard a cacophony of screeches and squawks in the woods across the road as we turned into the driveway. Closer investigation revealed a flock of wild turkeys making their noisy way through the autumn landscape.

Bonnie seated us in a cozy room that takes its name from its collection of *Gone With the Wind* memorabilia. Kerosene lamps flickered on the tables, a fireplace glowed, and live music (the mellow kind) set the tone for an enjoyable evening.

Our dinner started with an appetizer of Fried Mushrooms accompanied by Honey Mustard and Horseradish Sauces. Just as the mushrooms vanished, my husband's French Onion Soup appeared. His chin quivered when I asked to sample it—but how else was I to know how good it was? I let him taste my own hearty Ham and Corn Chowder.

Bread—baked and served in ceramic flowerpots—accompanied our entrees of Aged Rib-Eye Steak and Chicken Cordon Bleu, both popular menu items. Entrees come with the soup of the day or a garden salad.

We shared and savored a slice of the restaurant's specialty dessert, Strawberry Pizza. The flaky, pecan-studded crust covered with creamy filling and strawberry topping called for coffee—a perfect way to postpone dinner's end.

Stepping outside into the cold night—beautiful and silent—we decided that the neighborhood turkeys were asleep on their roosts. Or perhaps with Thanksgiving looming, they had conducted a caucus and voted to lower their noise level.

Cragsmere Manna's French Onion Soup

⅓ cup butter
4 cups onions, sliced thin
8 cups beef broth

½ cup croutons
8 slices Swiss cheese

Melt butter over medium heat. Add onions and cook until they turn a rich brown. Add broth and heat to boiling, stirring frequently. Reduce heat and simmer 10 minutes.

To serve, ladle into 8 bowls and add croutons and a slice of Swiss cheese to each bowl. Heat in a warm oven or microwave until cheese melts. Serves 8.

Cragsmere Manna's Ham and Corn Chowder

½ pound bacon
1 cup onions, chopped
1½ cups potatoes, peeled and
    diced
¾ cup celery, sliced
3 cups chicken broth

2½ cups whole kernel corn,
    drained
2 cups milk
1 cup ham, chopped
¼ cup parsley, chopped
1 teaspoon dried thyme
¼ teaspoon black pepper

Cook bacon to crisp stage in a large, heavy pot. Remove bacon; crumble and set aside. Pour off all but 1½ tablespoons drippings. In the same pot, cook onions, potatoes, and celery until tender. Add remaining ingredients and heat to a boil. Reduce heat to low; cover and simmer for 30 minutes. Serves 12.

Cragsmere Manna's Chicken Cordon Bleu

6 boneless chicken breasts
6 slices cooked ham
6 slices Swiss cheese
2 eggs, beaten
1 cup milk

1 cup flour
salt and pepper to taste
peanut oil
Cordon Bleu Sauce (recipe
    below)

Place chicken breasts between 2 sheets of waxed paper and flatten with a meat mallet. Place a slice of ham and a slice of cheese in the center of each breast. Roll up lengthwise and secure with toothpicks. Mix eggs and milk in a bowl. Combine flour and salt and pepper in a separate bowl. Dip chicken rolls in egg mixture, then roll in seasoned flour. Brown chicken rolls in peanut oil in a heavy skillet. Place in a baking dish and bake at 350 degrees for 40 to 45 minutes. If desired, serve over rice pilaf. Spoon Cordon Bleu Sauce over top. Serves 6.

Cordon Bleu Sauce

5 tablespoons butter

6 tablespoons flour
1 teaspoon salt

3 cups chicken broth

Melt butter in a saucepan. Add flour and salt and stir until smooth. Add broth and cook 3 to 5 minutes, stirring constantly. Yields 3 cups.

Log Cabin Restaurant and Deli

6080 Alabama 117
MENTONE

With its cool mountain temperatures—especially appealing before the advent of air conditioning—Mentone lured visitors from across the country. Perched on Lookout Mountain's brow at what is now the intersection of Alabama 117 and DeKalb County Road 89, this winsome village flourished as a fashionable summer resort town through the Gay Nineties. Some of the area's summer camps date back more than half a century. Both the Mentone Inn and the 1884 Mentone Springs Hotel—a three-story structure with turrets, dormers, and wraparound porches—make good bases for exploring the area.

Near the rambling hotel stands the Log Cabin Restaurant and Deli. Built between 1800 and 1835 for fur trading, the cabin might well have been frequented by Sequoyah—or so speculates Collette Kerby, who purchased the property more than a decade ago. Sequoyah moved to this part of Alabama as a young man. Inspired by what he called "white man's talking leaf," he created an alphabet for his people. Sequoyah Caverns, located nearby, were named in honor of this great Cherokee chief, as were California's giant trees and Sequoia National Park.

On the chilly day that my husband and I visited, flames danced in the cabin's rock fireplace and two comfortable Amish-made rocking chairs beckoned. Rocking proved a good way to take in the cabin's decor, from the walnut counter to the framed family photos to the mounted deer. The plank floors still show the marks where they were sawed, and close scrutiny revealed a few bullet holes in the original log walls. Mule bits function as door handles for the restrooms, and tugboat chains serve as handrails for the front-porch steps. Collette has extended the cabin's seating with a back porch that is open to the breezes during the summer and then converts to a closed-in dining room when temperatures drop.

Summer Hours
11:00 A.M. until 9:00 P.M.
Tuesday through Saturday

11:00 A.M. until 7:00 P.M.
Sunday

Winter Hours
11:00 A.M. until 7:00 P.M.
Tuesday through Thursday

11:00 A.M. until 9:00 P.M.
Friday and Saturday

No alcoholic beverages are served. For reservations, call (256) 634-4560.

My husband and I eased into a cozy, log-lined booth with leather backrests and studied the menu under a bushel-basket lamp. The blustery day called for a spot of Hot Spiced Tea, one of the Log Cabin's specialty drinks. This versatile beverage is also the basis for the popular Cabin Cooler, a refreshing drink with a nonalcoholic kick. Served in fruit jars, Cabin Coolers are a favorite with area camp counselors, according to Collette. A movie crew filming *Southern Heart* shot a scene of the cabin's interior with said beverage being served.

Collette, who honed her hostessing and culinary skills on hunting ranches in South Dakota and Nebraska, knows how to make people glad they stopped by. Her menu includes specialty sandwiches, salads, plate lunches, and dinner entrees with home-cooked vegetables and desserts.

A tasty cool-weather meal, the Chili Corn Pone features Southern cornbread topped with melted hot-pepper cheese, chili, grated cheddar, lettuce, tomato, sour cream, and nacho chips. The popular Country Ham with Red-Eye Gravy and the Country-Fried Steak come with a choice of two vegetables.

The deli's most sinful dessert, Hot Fudge Cake, makes a great afternoon snack. Sharing it with someone, as I did, divides the guilt (and the calories) and perhaps justifies sampling another favorite — in my case, the Log Cabin's delicious Peach Cobbler.

Log Cabin Restaurant and Deli's Hot Fudge Cake

Cake

4¾ cups flour	¼ cup butter, melted
3¾ cups sugar	1 cup oil
1 cup cocoa	2 cups water
dash of cinnamon	1 cup buttermilk
1 teaspoon vanilla extract	6 eggs

Combine dry ingredients, then stir in remaining items and mix until smooth. Pour into two 7- by 11-inch pans that have been sprayed with Pam. Bake in a preheated 325-degree oven for 25 to 30 minutes or until centers spring back when touched. Yields 2 cakes.

Icing

2 boxes confectioners' sugar
1 cup cocoa
dash of cinnamon
¼ cup butter, softened

¾ cup milk
1 teaspoon vanilla extract
pecan pieces

Combine sugar, cocoa, and cinnamon. Add all remaining ingredients except nuts; mixture should be thick but spreadable.

Spread on cakes and sprinkle with pecan pieces. If desired, microwave briefly to melt icing before serving.

Log Cabin Restaurant and Deli's Hot Tea Mix

2½ cups Lipton Instant Tea
    with Lemon mix
30 ounces Country Time
    Lemonade mix

1 cup Tang mix
¼ cup cinnamon
¼ cup cloves, ground

Mix all ingredients well and store in a dry container to use as needed.

When preparing Hot Tea, add 2 teaspoons of mixture to 1 cup of hot water and garnish with a lemon slice.

To make a Cabin Cooler, dissolve 2 teaspoons of Hot Tea Mix in ¼ cup water. Add ice and top with enough Sprite to fill glass. Garnish with a lemon slice.

THE GLOVER

Covington's

The Glover
524 Gunter Avenue
GUNTERSVILLE

"The opening of the $30,000 Hotel Glover only a few weeks ago will be one of Guntersville's most important events of 1933," reads an account from the local newspaper, the *Advertiser and Democrat*, dated December 27 of that year. In those days, Guntersville boasted many

paved streets, but enough dirt roads still existed to justify the purchase of a sprinkler for keeping down the dust, according to another newspaper item.

Guntersville is surrounded by a lake that didn't exist when the hotel was built. To create Lake Guntersville and its 69,100 acres of water, the Tennessee Valley Authority started moving families off the land in 1935. The lake-filling process, launched in January 1939, radically changed the area's appearance from farmland to waterscape and brought in watersports enthusiasts with its opportunities for boating, swimming, fishing, and other aquatic diversions.

The Glover's builder and a railroad colleague operated the hotel for more than two decades. Later, Marshall County bought the building and used it for public offices from the mid-1960s to the early 1980s. George Kappler purchased The Glover in 1984 and renovated it to house his company's corporate offices. While remodeling the second floor, Kappler's crew discovered a lift-up door leading to a concealed space between the floor joists, presumably used for liquor storage during Prohibition. A restaurant operated on the premises from 1987 to 1989, followed by another restaurant, Neena's, which later relocated to a lakeside property.

Today, The Glover houses several businesses, including Covington's, a great place for lunch. Reese Covington and his wife, Julia, came to Guntersville from Nashville, Tennessee, several years ago to start a cafe and a catering business. Before moving to the hotel, they prepared their "fabulous foods . . . with flair" a few doors up the street.

Covington's lunch menu of "soups, salads, and such" includes several heart-healthy selections. My favorite, the Downtowne Delight, consists of Chicken or Tuna Salad, a home-baked Muffin, Pimento Cheese on rye, fresh fruit, and a choice of veggies or Pasta Salad. And

I always order the Towne Tea Punch, a fruity iced tea.

The delectable desserts include "The Brownie," Gooey Butter Bars, and assorted tarts—Derby, Buttermilk Chess, and Lemon. Reese shared recipes for his delicious Petite Butter Cookies with Lemon Curd, Chutney Chicken Salad, and savory Apricot-Rosemary Pork Tenderloin.

Covington's Chutney Chicken Salad

3 cups chicken breast, cooked and chopped
½ cup golden raisins
1 cup celery, chopped
3 hard-boiled eggs, diced
¼ cup pecans, chopped
1 teaspoon fresh parsley, chopped
¼ teaspoon salt

¼ teaspoon pepper
¼ teaspoon curry powder
½ cup mayonnaise
⅓ cup sour cream
2 tablespoons mango chutney (commercial)
½ teaspoon prepared chicken base (commercial)

Mix chicken with raisins, celery, eggs, pecans, parsley, salt, and pepper. In a separate bowl, stir together curry powder, mayonnaise, sour cream, chutney, and chicken base, blending thoroughly. Add dressing to chicken mixture, stirring until well blended. If desired, serve on fresh sliced tomatoes atop a bed of crisp leaf lettuce, or fill cocktail-size cream puffs or pastry shells for wonderful hors d'oeuvres. Yields 6 cups.

Covington's Apricot-Rosemary Pork Tenderloin

3-pound boneless pork loin
8-ounce jar apricot preserves
½ cup white wine
    Worcestershire sauce
¼ cup olive oil
½ teaspoon white pepper

1 teaspoon garlic, chopped
1 teaspoon rosemary, dried or fresh
1 teaspoon parsley flakes
salt to taste

Place pork in a container for marinating. Combine remaining ingredients in a saucepan until thoroughly heated. Reserve ½ cup marinade for sauce. Pour remaining marinade over pork, turning to coat all sides. Allow to marinate in refrigerator 8 to 12 hours, turning meat once.

Remove meat from marinade and place on a roasting rack in a baking pan. Roast in a preheated 300-degree oven for 1½ to 2 hours. Allow to cool slightly, slice, and serve with reserved marinade. Serves 10 to 12.

Note: Covington's prepares this both as an entree and as hors d'oeuvres, sliced in smaller pieces and served on Jalapeño Corn Muffins.

Covington's Petite Butter Cookies with Lemon Curd

Cookies

5 cups all-purpose flour
1 cup sugar

2 cups butter, softened (no substitutes)

Combine flour and sugar in a mixing bowl. Work butter in little by little with hands until a soft dough forms. Pinch off 1-teaspoon portions of dough and roll into balls. Flatten and place 1 inch apart on a parchment-lined baking pan. Bake at 325 degrees until lightly browned on the edges. Cool. Yields 50 to 60 cookies.

Lemon Curd

2 cups sugar
1 fresh lemon with seeds removed, ground in food processor

¼ cup lemon juice
¾ cup butter
6 eggs

Place first 4 ingredients in top of a double boiler and melt completely. Beat eggs and add to lemon mixture. Stir over heat until mixture is thick and coats a wooden spoon. Allow to cool.

Serve in a compote container as an accompaniment to Petite Butter Cookies.

Bubba's

109 Washington Street
HUNTSVILLE

*K*nown today as the birth-place of America's space program, Huntsville served as an early capital of Alabama. Delegates met here to draft the state's first constitution in 1819.

Today, Huntsville continues to play a strategic role in the nation's space program but preserves its past as well. Alabama Constitution Village, Harrison Brothers Hardware Store, and other downtown sites provide glimpses into the early years, before the town mushroomed into today's metropolis.

11:00 A.M. until 10:00 P.M.
Monday and Tuesday

11:00 A.M. until 11:00 P.M.
Wednesday through Saturday

The bar closes later, depending on the crowd.

For reservations (recommended on weekends), call (256) 534-3133.

Exploring the attractions around the courthouse square can help you work up a hearty appetite, and Bubba's makes an ideal stop for a lunch break. Located in the heart of the historic district, it occupies a painted brick building with canopied windows. The structure once housed a turn-of-the-century hotel upstairs and several businesses on the ground level.

Posters from Huntsville's annual outdoor arts festival line the walls over Bubba's waist-high beaded-board woodwork. A green-and-pink color scheme predominates in the dining rooms. An enclosed rear courtyard with wrought-iron tables and hanging ferns offers a pleasant backdrop for dining when weather permits. On the back brick wall, a large mural depicts a beach scene.

At lunchtime, Bubba's draws a mix of folks, from families to travelers to career types. Its casual ambiance and sports-bar atmosphere also attract the singles crowd for drinks, dinner, and live entertainment on weekends.

Owner Bubba Conner, a third-generation Huntsvillian, started cooking at the age of six. After working in real estate, auto repair, and construction, he turned his talents to the food business, operating both restaurants and a broad-based catering operation.

"If you can eat it, I can cook it," said Bubba, who sometimes prepares wild-game dinners for small groups. He also does such things as

Caviar-Covered Canapés, Lobster Bisque, and ice sculptures for special catering events.

Bubba's serves delicious appetizers like Hot Artichoke and Spinach Dip, salads, and award-winning Fajitas. The daily luncheon specials feature a variety of vegetables accompanied by iced tea in frosted fruit jars. Bubba's specialty is Southern-Style Ribs, which come char-broiled, steamed in beer, and slathered in a special Barbecue Sauce.

After sharing his recipe for Chili, Bubba promised me, "It's great. Won't be a drop left."

Bubba's Twice-Cooked Potato Casserole

6 large potatoes
2 cups cheddar cheese, shredded
½ cup margarine, melted
2 cups sour cream

1 cup bacon, fried and crumbled
1 teaspoon salt
½ teaspoon pepper
½ cup green onions, diced fine

Boil potatoes in the skins. Let cool, then peel and chop. Combine potatoes with remaining ingredients and stir lightly. Place in a buttered baking dish and bake for 30 minutes at 350 degrees. Serves 8.

Bubba's Chili

1 pound ground chuck
2 pounds smoked sausage, sliced
2 medium onions, chopped
1 bell pepper, chopped
2 16-ounce cans pinto beans, undrained
2 16-ounce cans red kidney beans, undrained

¼ cup chili powder
1 teaspoon black pepper
1 teaspoon garlic salt
1 teaspoon salt
½ teaspoon red pepper
2 tablespoons flour
6 cups water

Sauté ground chuck, sausage, onions, and bell pepper until meat is done. Drain grease and add remaining ingredients. Cover and simmer 1 hour, stirring occasionally to prevent sticking. If desired, serve with crackers and shredded cheese. Serves 12.

Johnston Street Cafe

115 Johnston Street Southeast
DECATUR

$\mathcal{D}$ecatur audiences once flocked to the Old Cotaco Opera House, (erected in 1890) for musical performances, pageants, and spirited vaudeville shows. After the country's top touring acts stopped singing, juggling, and tap-dancing their way across the stage, the Johnston Street structure settled into its identity as the Old Masonic Building, where couples danced to big-band sounds. More than a decade ago, Barbara and Wally Inscho and Marella and Jim Adams restored the historic brick structure for commercial use.

8:30 A.M. until 5:30 P.M.
Monday through Friday

11:00 A.M. until 2:00 P.M.
Saturday

Dinner
6:00 P.M. until 10:00 P.M.
Thursday through Saturday

For reservations,
call (256) 350-6715.

A side entrance on the building's lower level leads to the Johnston Street Cafe, a Tuscan-style bistro and deli. The cafe offers traditional Southern fare and eclectic upscale cuisine in an attractive setting with a color scheme of white, gray, and dusty rose. Patrons can enjoy lunch or dinner on the premises, purchase the makings of a picnic, or order dinner to go. Or they can opt for a meal in the cafe's courtyard, weather permitting.

Chef Scott Curry apprenticed at Atlanta's Ritz-Carlton, trained two years under a French master chef, and served as sous-chef at Decatur Country Club before taking over Johnston Street Cafe, formerly owned and operated by Betty Sims. "Basically, I take traditional dishes and put new flair into them by using fusion and an eclectic approach," Curry said. "I try to present good cuisine at a reasonable rate and offer good wines."

The lunch menu includes homemade soups, salads, sandwiches, and desserts. The daily special might be Shrimp Creole, Chicken Divan, Stuffed Bruschetta, Meatloaf, Lasagna, or Shrimp Salad.

As a prelude to dinner, I sampled the cafe's Spring Rolls, served with Japanese Mustard and Plum Sauce, and felt duty-bound to help a dining companion consume his Escargots with Baby Mixed Greens and French Bread Toast Points. The Johnston Street Prawns, stuffed with spicy Monterey Jack and wrapped in smoked bacon, make a savory appetizer, too.

For my entree, I chose the herb-crusted, pan-seared Citrus Halibut. The Crab Cakes, the Roasted Rack of Lamb with Black Olive Sauce, and the marinated, grilled Calvados Pork Tenderloin rank high on the list of favorites here also.

Although the former opera house no longer offers vaudeville, you can book a table for a fine dinner at Johnston Street Cafe and end your evening with a standing-ovation dessert like Bananas Foster or Crème Brûlée.

Johnston Street Cafe's Roasted Rack of Lamb with Black Olive Sauce

Lamb

1 lamb rack, chine and fat
   cap removed
2 tablespoons virgin olive oil

1 sprig rosemary, stemmed
   and chopped
salt and pepper to taste

Rub lamb rack with olive oil and season generously with rosemary and salt and pepper. Add a few drops of oil to a roasting pan and heat pan on stove until very hot. Sear lamb on all sides until brown. Turn lamb bone side down and roast on grill until desired degree of doneness. (Medium-rare takes about 10 minutes.) Allow lamb to cool about 10 minutes at room temperature, then slice into 8 chops. Serves 4.

Note: You can also finish lamb in a 325-degree oven. Insert meat thermometer and remove lamb at 160 degrees for medium doneness.

Black Olive Sauce

½ cup unsalted butter
4 cloves garlic, peeled and
   crushed
4 shallots, peeled and chopped
1½ teaspoons black
   peppercorns
1 cup Madeira

1 cup red wine
1 sprig rosemary
½ tomato, seeded and diced
½ cup brown roux
¼ cup pitted Niçoise olives,
   chopped
salt and pepper to taste

Melt ½ tablespoon butter in a saucepan. Sauté garlic, shallots, and peppercorns until lightly browned. Add Madeira, red wine, rosemary, and tomato and simmer until reduced by ⅔. Add brown roux and return to a boil. Turn off heat and slowly whisk in remaining butter until incorporated. Strain sauce, then purée until almost smooth. Add olives and season with salt and pepper. Reserve on a warm plate until ready to serve over Roasted Rack of Lamb.

Johnston Street Cafe's Wilted Spinach and Bacon Salad

2 pounds fresh spinach,
   trimmed to yield 1 pound
6 slices bacon
3 tablespoons brown sugar
apple cider vinegar to taste

4 large mushrooms, sliced
2 hard-boiled eggs, diced
¾ cup sweet pickles, chopped
salt and pepper to taste

Wash spinach and pat dry. Cook bacon in a skillet over medium-low heat until crisp. Drain on paper towels. Strain bacon drippings through a fine sieve, wipe out skillet with a paper towel, and return drippings to skillet. Add brown sugar and stir over low heat until dissolved, then add vinegar. Toss with spinach, mushrooms, eggs, pickles, and crumbled bacon in a salad bowl. Season with salt and pepper. Serves 6.

Shelley's Iron Gate

402 Johnston Street
DECATUR

$\mathcal{W}$hen you visit Shelley's Iron Gate, you won't see the name-sake ironwork, because it remains at the restaurant's original location in another part of Decatur. What you will find is a lovely, butter-colored brick mansion with green awnings and shutters. Built by Judge William E. Skeggs, who moved from Huntsville to Decatur in

Lunch
11:00 A.M. until 2:00 P.M.
Monday through Saturday

For reservations (recommended for parties of five or more), call (256) 350-6795.

1871, the Queen Anne–style house dates to the early 1900s and was once part of a large estate. The structure later served as an apartment house.

In 1987, Betty Shelley converted the historic home into a restaurant, which she sold to Cindy Sensenberger in 1991. Cindy had previously operated a restaurant in Canada for several years. Upon returning to her native Huntsville, she discovered the Decatur restaurant for sale and seized the opportunity.

"Several of my family members are in the restaurant profession," Cindy said. "I guess it runs in the family, and I've always wanted a restaurant in an old house."

Shelley's exudes Victorian ambiance throughout its eight dining rooms. Special features include a handsome staircase in the foyer, hardwood floors, three fireplaces, original doors, and fourteen-foot ceilings.

Cindy retained several menu items from the traditional tearoom bill of fare and also incorporated some things of her own. Among the old favorites are Strawberry Pretzel Salad, Chicken and Broccoli Casserole, and Poulet de Normandy, which consists of baked chicken and dressing in a cheese and mushroom sauce. The menu might feature Shrimp Gumbo, Crunchy Chicken Casserole, and Vegetable Lasagna. Yeast Rolls and side dishes like Marinated Carrots and Cranberry Congealed Salad accompany the entrees. Sandwiches, soups, salads, and desserts are also available.

Cindy shared recipes for her delicious Seafood Creole Casserole and a dessert that conjures up jukebox music and soda fountains — Banana Split Pie.

After lunch, consider walking off some calories in nearby Mooresville, a town that dates to 1818 and is thus one year older than the state of Alabama itself. Listed on the National Register of Historic Places, this charming village is populated by sixty families and occupies an area of one square mile.

Strolling along streets lined by picket fences, wild hydrangea, and splendid old shade trees, you'll see a variety of vintage structures, including churches, lovely Federal-style homes, the Stagecoach Inn, and Mooresville's post office, a wee, weathered-poplar, tin-roofed building that dates from around 1840.

Shelley's Iron Gate's Seafood Creole Casserole

1 cup onions, chopped
½ cup celery, chopped
½ cup green pepper, chopped
½ cup green onions, chopped
½ cup parsley, chopped
1½ tablespoons garlic, chopped
2 tablespoons butter
1½ cups shrimp
1½ cups lump crabmeat
2½ cups cooked rice
2 cans cream of mushroom soup
2 drops Tabasco sauce
2 tablespoons Worcestershire sauce
1½ teaspoons Creole seasoning

Sauté onions, celery, green pepper, green onions, parsley, and garlic in butter until soft. Combine vegetable mixture with remaining ingredients in a 3-quart casserole dish and mix well. Bake at 350 degrees for 25 to 30 minutes. Serves 8 to 10.

Shelley's Iron Gate's Banana Split Pie

10-ounce package frozen
  sliced strawberries
½ cup sugar
3 tablespoons unflavored
  gelatin
½ cup cold water
2 cups plain yogurt
2 tablespoons strawberry
  extract

½ cup crushed pineapple,
  drained
2 bananas, mashed
16 ounces Cool Whip
2 chocolate piecrusts
whipped topping
chocolate sauce
strawberry topping
pecan pieces

Combine strawberries, sugar, gelatin, and water in a saucepan over low heat, stirring constantly until sugar dissolves. Remove from heat, pour into a large stainless-steel bowl, and whip in yogurt, strawberry extract, pineapple, and bananas. Place bowl in an ice bath to cool. When mixture begins to set, fold in Cool Whip. Spoon mixture into piecrusts and refrigerate at least 3 hours. Before serving, top each piece with whipped topping, chocolate sauce, strawberry topping, and pecan pieces. Yields 2 pies.

Simp McGhee's

725 Bank Street Northeast
DECATUR

$\mathscr{A}$pproaching Simp Mc-Ghee's for dinner, I admired Decatur's venerable Old State Bank, a Civil War survivor that commands a lofty position at the end of Bank Street. Located a short stroll away, the restaurant occupies a storefront that dates to the late 1800s, as do many of the antique shops and galleries along Bank Street.

This saloon-style eatery takes its name from a colorful turn-of-the-century riverboat captain, William Simpson McGhee, a master pilot who made regular runs between Decatur and Chattanooga. Although Simp died in 1917, tales of his whiskey-running exploits live on. Along with running a shipping business and operating his nearby Bank Street saloon (where legend says he kept a beer-drinking pig on the premises), Simp found time to indulge his passion for playing pranks. He also found time to visit Decatur's famous madam, a redhead known as Miss Kate. According to local lore, Simp always announced his arrival via riverboat by blowing a steam whistle, which alerted Miss Kate that he would soon be at her door—and also signaled any other guests to make their departure.

In 1986, Ginnie Lind and Bob Riddle transformed a former dry-goods store into a restaurant that practically demanded to be called Simp McGhee's. Housed in an 1894 two-story red-brick structure close to the sites of Miss Kate's establishment and Simp's saloon, the restaurant features a pressed-tin ceiling, original flooring and fixtures, and a handsome wooden bar. The bar is fronted by a row of red-seated stools. Its top and its brass rail came from Simp's own tavern—and perhaps continue to inspire the pub's lively atmosphere today.

On my way to the more sedate upstairs dining room, I admired the various painted figures standing about—Confederate and Union soldiers, George Washington, an Indian, and others. Bob carved them all by hand.

Nibbling on crispy French Bread Medallions with some of Chef Dean Moore's toppings, I contemplated which of Simp's savory seafood and Cajun specialties to order. One of Dean's signature dishes is Snapper

Pontchartrain, topped with bay shrimp, crabmeat, mushrooms, and green onions. It sounded too good to pass up—and fortunately, I didn't. Other popular entrees include Cajun Shrimp Sauté, Blackened Snapper, Jambalaya, Shrimp Dijon, and Stuffed Gulf Flounder, as well as pasta, poultry, and beef entrees.

With its praline flavor, the Bananas Julian hints of New Orleans and is a grand way to conclude a meal. I couldn't wait to make this delightful dessert at home—for my next dinner party.

Simp McGhee's Snapper Pontchartrain

1 teaspoon salt
½ teaspoon red pepper
½ teaspoon white pepper
6 6- to 8-ounce red snapper
   fillets
2 bunches green onions,
   chopped, both white and
   green parts
4-ounce can sliced
   mushrooms, drained

4 tablespoons roasted red bell
   pepper, diced
½ cup unsalted butter
¼ cup dry white wine
8 ounces jumbo lump
   crabmeat
8 ounces small salad shrimp,
   cooked
6 cups cooked rice

Preheat oven to 400 degrees. Combine salt, red pepper, and white pepper and sprinkle on fillets. Bake fish 15 to 20 minutes until it flakes. While fish is baking, sauté onions, mushrooms, and bell pepper in butter. Add wine, crabmeat, and shrimp and warm through.

Place fish over cooked rice and top with crab and shrimp mixture. If desired, serve with drawn butter. Serves 6.

Note: This recipe works equally well with grouper or most any flaky white fish.

Simp McGhee's Shrimp Dijon

1 cup milk
1 egg
1½ cups flour
salt and pepper to taste

14 jumbo shrimp, peeled and
    deveined, tails removed
½ cup butter
⅓ cup Dijon mustard
⅓ cup green onion tops, chopped

Combine milk and egg. Season flour with salt and pepper. Dust shrimp in flour mixture. Dip in egg wash, then back in flour. Heat butter in a nonstick skillet over medium-high heat. Place shrimp in butter, brown both sides, and remove. Lower heat, wipe out skillet, and place back on heat. Dab one side of each shrimp with ½ teaspoon mustard. Place shrimp in skillet mustard side down. Dab other side with ½ teaspoon mustard and turn again. Gently toss with green onions and remove to a serving dish. Serves 2.

Simp McGhee's Bananas Julian

½ cup unsalted butter
½ cup plus 2
    tablespoons light
    brown sugar

¼ teaspoon vanilla
3 tablespoons dark rum
2 bananas, sliced
vanilla ice cream

Melt butter in a saucepan. Add sugar and stir until smooth. Add vanilla and rum and mix well. Add bananas. Place ice cream in chilled bowls and top with sauce. Serves 4.

Court Street Cafe

201 North Seminary Street
FLORENCE

$\mathcal{W}$hen I first visited Florence, the brick plaza in front of Court Street Cafe teemed with crowds in town for a week of swinging jazz during the annual W. C. Handy Music Festival. Each August, the city becomes a mecca for jazz lovers, who come for the parades, jam sessions, concerts featuring celebrated musicians, picnics, the DaDooRunRun for joggers, and the colorful Street Strut led by the Grand Oobeedoo.

11:00 A.M. until 10:00 P.M.
Sunday through Thursday

11:00 A.M. until 11:00 P.M.
Friday and Saturday

Reservations are not accepted. For information, call (256) 767-4300.

Court Street Cafe occupies a corner building that dates back half a century. At various times, it has served as a drugstore, a restaurant, a bar, and a stamp redemption store. During its drugstore days, youngsters would come in clutching coins for limeade and penny candy after taking in a movie across the street at The Shoals Theater, which opened its doors in 1948.

With a ceiling of embossed tin, brass rails, pub tables, and two dining levels, the two-hundred-seat cafe offers a casual, easygoing atmosphere and a dash of nostalgia.

"We wanted something synonymous with downtown Florence," said owner Jake Jacobs when asked about the cafe's name. Jake offers a rotating seasonal menu. Most of Court Street's recipes were developed at the restaurant and perfected by trial and error, he explained. He calls the cuisine "contemporary American."

Operating on the premise that little things count, the staff grinds beans for the cafe's coffee, squeezes fresh oranges for juice, and presents each visiting child with a balloon, a coloring book, crayons, animal crackers, or other treats.

The cafe's noteworthy Grilled Chicken Salad features mixed greens covered with Monterey Jack cheese, diced tomatoes, scallions, almonds, fresh fruit, and sliced chicken. The popular Oriental Salad consists of fresh Chinese cabbage, almonds, Sesame Peanut Sauce, soy-marinated chicken, and mandarin oranges. Court Street's Honey Mustard Dressing makes a tangy dip for fresh vegetables.

Jake provided enticing recipes for Garlic-Rubbed Tenderloin with Roasted Red Pepper Sauce and Cream of Artichoke Soup. The Garlic-Rubbed Tenderloin was Jake's idea, though the chef suggested some embellishments. Other favorites include Lemon Basil Tuna, served either grilled or blackened, and Prime Rib with Creamy Horseradish Sauce. The Prime Rib is available on weekends.

The Caramel Nut Brownie and Apple Crunch Pie with French Vanilla Ice Cream prove ever popular.

And by the way, Court Street Cafe is *not* on Court Street.

Court Street Cafe's Cream of Artichoke Soup

½ cup butter
1 tablespoon garlic, chopped
4 cups artichoke hearts,
*   chopped coarse*
½ cup carrots, shredded
½ cup mushrooms, sliced
1½ cups onions, chopped

1½ cups flour
2 quarts chicken broth
3 cups heavy cream
1½ teaspoons white pepper
1½ teaspoons parsley,
*   chopped*
1 cup croutons

Melt butter in a large skillet and sauté garlic, artichokes, carrots, mushrooms, and onions until onions are translucent. Add flour; stir over medium heat until there are no bubbles from flour. Transfer to a soup pot, add chicken broth, and mix well. Bring mixture to a boil and let boil for 10 minutes. Reduce heat to simmer. Add heavy cream, white pepper, and parsley and mix well. Allow soup to simmer until thick. Garnish with croutons before serving. Serves 10 to 12.

Court Street Cafe's Garlic-Rubbed Tenderloin with Roasted Red Pepper Sauce

Tenderloin

¼ cup olive oil
½ cup garlic, chopped
6 6-ounce beef fillets
⅓ cup black pepper
2 tablespoons kosher salt

1 tablespoon dried basil
*   flakes*
1 teaspoon dried tarragon
*   flakes*

Combine olive oil and garlic and rub into fillets. Combine dry ingredients and sprinkle over fillets. Let stand for 2 hours in refrigerator, then grill to desired doneness. Serves 6.

Roasted Red Pepper Sauce

3 pounds red peppers
2 tablespoons yellow onions, chopped
1 tablespoon butter
2 tablespoons flour
1 quart heavy cream
1 cup milk

1½ teaspoons Paul Prudhomme's Cajun Magic
1½ teaspoons garlic, chopped
1½ teaspoons salt
¼ teaspoon white pepper

Blacken skin of peppers by placing them on a fork and holding them over open flame on stove. Cool peppers and cut in half from stem to end. Remove stems and seeds. Remove skins by running cold water over peppers. Place peppers and onions in blender and purée. Melt the butter in a skillet and add flour; cook the roux until there are no bubbles, but do not let it turn dark. Add heavy cream and milk, then simmer until mixture begins to thicken. Remove from heat. Add pepper purée, then all remaining spices. Mix thoroughly.

Top fillets with Red Pepper Sauce and serve.

Trowbridge's

316 North Court Street
FLORENCE

*O*n his way from his Texas home to a dairy farmers' convention in North Carolina in 1917, Paul Trowbridge passed through Florence. He liked the place so much that he returned with his family and purchased property. In 1918, he built

9:00 A.M. until 5:30 P.M.
Monday through Saturday

For information,
call (256) 764-1503.

Trowbridge's Creamery, where local farmers brought their milk and cream to be processed. The family occupied the second floor over the ice cream shop, and the dairy stood behind it. Paul's original recipe for Orange-Pineapple Ice Cream still proves a hit today.

When his grandfather established the business in downtown Florence, says current owner Don Trowbridge, it was one of only two buildings on the block. After his dad, Donald Sr., went to war, his mother, Martha, ran Trowbridge's. In fact, it was she who introduced the homemade Chili in 1944. In developing her recipe, Martha made batches of Chili and requested input from customers as she refined it. Her recipe remains a guarded secret.

When Don left his job as a computer systems analyst in Virginia to take over the family business, he made only two changes—he purchased a new cash register "to replace the crank kind" and added Ham and Biscuits for the downtown crowd, "who wanted a bite for breakfast," as he put it. The latter change caused his manager to rebel. She said she had enough to do without making Biscuits every morning.

So Don made them himself—and collected quite a few compliments in the process. After hearing customers praise her boss's Biscuits, the manager challenged, "I can make better Biscuits than you."

A third-generation owner, Don attributes Trowbridge's longevity to keeping the menu simple—sandwiches, salads, soups, Chili, and ice cream. A mirrored soda fountain lists ice cream flavors and drink choices. The Oh My Gosh dessert—named for the response it almost always elicits from customers—is a brownie piled high with Vanilla Ice Cream and topped with hot caramel, whipped cream, and a cherry.

A large painting on the rear wall shows that Trowbridge's interior has remained virtually unchanged through the years. Posters from past festivals pay tribute to local natives Helen Keller and W. C. Handy, "the Father of the Blues." Framed photos depict scenes from early

Florence and the construction of Wilson Dam, which began as a World War I project to supply power for making munitions.

Indeed, Trowbridge's has been called "Florence's definitive business." Sipping coffee, I listened as a group of regulars sat at a back table critiquing current events. One can learn a lot about Florence at Trowbridge's—and enjoy Orange-Pineapple Ice Cream, too.

Trowbridge's Chicken and Rice Soup

9 cups chicken broth
¼ cup uncooked rice
¼ cup carrots, grated coarse
½ cup onions, chopped coarse

2 cups chicken breast, cut
* into bite-size pieces*
6 sprigs fresh parsley,
* chopped*
salt and pepper to taste

Bring broth to a boil in a large saucepan over high heat. Add rice, carrots, onions, and chicken. Simmer covered for 20 minutes. Add parsley and salt and pepper. Serves 8.

Trowbridge's Egg and Olive Salad

12 hard-boiled eggs, diced
1 cup mayonnaise

1 cup stuffed green olives,
* sliced*
salt and pepper to taste

Combine all ingredients. Refrigerate several hours to allow flavors to blend. Serves 8 to 12.

Note: For a delicious variation, add ⅛ cup of minced fresh dill.

LOUISIANA The Restaurant

406 North Montgomery Avenue
SHEFFIELD

If you love the cuisine of New Orleans (and who doesn't?), you'll enjoy Matthew Wood's restaurant, LOUISI-ANA. Located on Montgomery Avenue between Fourth and Fifth Streets, it occupies the street level of a three-story brick structure built around 1888.

Through the decades, this building has been home to a tailor, a shirtmaker, an architect, a real-estate dealer, a dentist, an attorney, a wallpaper merchant, a photographer, furniture dealers, physicians, surgeons, and funeral directors. In its current incarnation as a restaurant, peach and white accents complement a hunter-green setting with ivy-covered latticework. Mardi Gras memorabilia and the work of local artists and photographers are on display.

Originally from New Orleans, Matthew boasts impressive culinary credentials from Antoine's, Upperline, and other fine restaurants. In LOUISIANA's spacious quarters, he and his wife, Pat, present a repertoire of Acadian, Creole, and Southern favorites like Shrimp Creole, Gumbo, Jambalaya, Etouffée, and Shrimp and Corn Chowder.

Matthew's Gumbo and his Crab-Stuffed Mushrooms both make great beginnings. The house specialties include Fish Conti, a seafood-and-pasta dish called Shrimp and Crawfish Virginia, Beef Medallions, Pork Loin Bordelaise, spicy Shrimp Louisiana, and Seafood Eggplant Pirogue, which consists of eggplant halves hollowed out, heaped with crabmeat, crawfish, and shrimp, and then topped with Dill Sauce. Another favorite, Chicken Lafayette, is often requested by regulars, and it's easy to understand why. When you make this dish at home, you'll collect plenty of accolades, too. A bonus is that the accompanying Cajun Spice Mixture can be kept on hand for next time — and next time may roll around sooner than you think!

Lunch
11:00 A.M. until 2:00 P.M.
Tuesday through Thursday

Dinner
5:00 P.M. until 9:00 P.M.
Tuesday through Thursday

5:00 P.M. until 10:00 P.M.
Friday and Saturday

Buffet
11:00 A.M. until 2:00 P.M.
Sunday

For reservations (recommended at lunch for parties of five or more and at dinner), call (256) 386-0801.

The desserts here are truly inspired, so plan on indulging in something wonderfully wicked. Quite often, the dessert tray features Banana Coconut Rum Cake (Matthew's recipe made the pages of *Bon Appétit*), Almond Amaretto Cake, and Grand Marnier Cheesecake. Matthew shared his marvelous recipe for LOUISIANA's ever-popular Piña Colada Cheesecake with Sour Cream Topping, so you can enjoy it at home.

LOUISIANA The Restaurant's Chicken Lafayette

4 6-ounce boneless, skinless chicken breasts
3 tablespoons Cajun Spice Mixture (recipe below)
½ cup white wine
4 tablespoons lemon juice
1 tablespoon shallots, minced
½ cup andouille sausage, diced small

2 cups heavy whipping cream
½ cup plus 2 tablespoons butter
2 teaspoons garlic, chopped
1 teaspoon salt
1 cup crawfish tail meat
2 tablespoons green onion, minced
1 teaspoon parsley flakes
1 teaspoon white pepper

Season chicken breasts by rubbing with 2 tablespoons of Cajun Spice Mixture, then set aside. Combine wine, lemon juice, and shallots in a small saucepan. Reduce on medium heat until only 3 teaspoons of liquid remain. Add sausage and whipping cream. Reduce by half on medium heat. Meanwhile, melt 2 tablespoons butter in a medium-sized skillet. Add chicken breasts and cook over medium heat about 4 minutes on each side until done. Place chicken on serving plate. Add garlic, salt, crawfish, green onion, parsley, pepper, and remaining 1 tablespoon Cajun Spice Mixture to skillet. Bring back to a boil and whisk in remaining ½ cup butter a small square at a time. Spoon sauce over chicken and serve. Serves 4.

Cajun Spice Mixture

½ cup oregano leaves
½ cup garlic powder
½ cup cayenne pepper
¼ cup paprika
1 tablespoon ground
  cumin

¼ cup thyme leaves
¼ cup onion powder
1 tablespoon black pepper
¼ cup salt
1½ teaspoons white pepper

Mix well and store in an airtight container. Yields about 2 cups.

LOUISIANA The Restaurant's Piña Colada Cheesecake with Sour Cream Topping

Cheesecake

4 8-ounce packages cream
  cheese, softened
1 cup sugar
¼ cup Coco Lopez
¼ cup light rum
1½ teaspoons vanilla extract

1½ cups crushed pineapple,
  drained
½ cup coconut, shredded
3 whole eggs
2 egg yolks

Beat cream cheese and sugar in a mixer until smooth. Add Coco Lopez, rum, vanilla, pineapple, and coconut and mix well. Add eggs and egg yolks and mix until just blended. Pour into a 9-inch springform pan and bake in center of oven for 55 minutes at 350 degrees. Remove from oven and let cool 15 minutes.

Topping

2 cups sour cream
¼ cup plus two tablespoons
  Coco Lopez

¼ cup light rum
¾ cup sugar
1½ teaspoons vanilla

Combine all ingredients. Pour over cheesecake and bake for 5 minutes at 350 degrees. Remove from oven and let cool at least 6 hours before serving. Serves 12.

Provence Market

105 First Avenue Northeast
CULLMAN

$\mathcal{C}$ullman, with its downtown streets said to be "four beer wagons wide," dates to 1873, when Colonel John G. Cullmann bought a large tract of land and established a colony for German immigrants that subsequently attracted ten thousand settlers to northern Alabama. A replica of the founder's Bavarian-style home (which burned in 1912) houses the Cullman County Museum, whose ex-

hibits of furniture, china, jewelry, clothing, early tools, and a beer wagon showcase the city's German heritage.

Located nearby, Provence Market serves tea, coffee, dessert, and lunch — but no beer. Partners Kim Calvert and Kerry Quinn met as carpooling mothers and soon discovered that they had other mutual interests. For more than two years, they searched for the perfect place for the restaurant they envisioned. Then along came the opportunity to acquire Provence Market in Cullman's historic warehouse district.

Originally opened by Carson and Wendy Glasscock, the cafe sold breads, fruits, and specialty coffees and also offered daily lunch specials. The inspiration for the venture was a bicycling trip through the south of France that Carson took after completing college. Intrigued by the country's open-air markets, he wanted to establish an eatery back home that had the flavor of Provence.

Provence Market occupies a corner section of a warehouse built around 1900. Previously, the structure housed various businesses, including a wholesale operation that supplied peddlers and country stores. Original windows, a pressed-tin ceiling, and an antique oak double desk once used for warehouse transactions lend a touch of yesteryear. The cafe's two dining rooms seat thirty-six, but plans are in the works to transform the open side area into a courtyard for patio dining.

Sitting at a table covered with a blue-and-white-plaid cloth, my husband and I sipped coffee and shared a White Chocolate Brownie and a slice of Ribbon Cake while chatting with Kim and Kerry.

Chef Kerry enjoys living in Cullman because of its small-town atmosphere. She started mincing and sautéeing her way through recipes as a college student in Connecticut. After marriage and motherhood limited her schedule, she launched a home-based catering operation that continued through moves to Pennsylvania, California, and Atlanta. "My food has a healthy focus," she confided, "but don't tell the men."

"We want people to stop by for lunch or coffee and dessert and then take home dinner," added Kim, who brought fifteen years of experience as a wedding director and caterer with her to Provence Market.

The lunch menu offers homemade soups, salads, pasta selections, sandwiches, and home-baked desserts. A weekly dinner—offered on Fridays—features such entrees as locally grown Quail and Free-Range Chicken. Although the cafe does not serve alcohol, brown-bagging is permitted.

After dining at Provence Market, you might want to visit Cullman's east side for a Lilliputian world tour at Ave Maria Grotto, located on the grounds of a Benedictine monastery. This unique garden features more than 150 miniature reproductions of famous landmarks created by a gifted monk, Brother Joseph Zoettl.

Provence Market's Sauerkraut Salad

1¾ cups sugar
1 cup vinegar
28-ounce can shredded sauerkraut, drained and rinsed
¼ cup red onion, chopped fine

½ cup green pepper, chopped coarse
2 ribs celery with strings removed, chopped fine
12 to 18 stuffed green olives, chopped coarse

Combine sugar and vinegar in a saucepan. Bring to a boil, stirring occasionally. Remove from heat and let cool. Combine sauerkraut, onion, green pepper, celery, and olives in a nonmetallic bowl. Pour dressing over vegetables, toss, and chill well. Keeps well for several days if covered and refrigerated. Serves 6 to 8.

Provence Market's Broccoli Cornbread

4 eggs, beaten until foamy
8½-ounce box Jiffy corn
muffin mix
⅓ cup butter, melted
¾ cup sour cream

1 small onion, chopped fine
1½ cups fresh or frozen
broccoli, cooked and
chopped

Combine ingredients and pour into a buttered 9- by 5- by 3-inch loaf pan. Bake at 350 degrees for 40 minutes or until lightly browned; center should spring back when touched. Yields 1 loaf.

Provence Market's White Chocolate Brownies

1 cup butter
10 ounces white baking chips
1¼ cups sugar
4 eggs

2 cups flour
¼ teaspoon salt
1 cup pecans, broken and
lightly toasted

Place butter and white chips in a large mixing bowl. Melt in a microwave, stirring until smooth. Add remaining ingredients and mix well. Line a 9- by 13-inch baking pan with greased foil and pour in batter. Bake at 325 degrees for 30 minutes or until lightly browned and until center is set; do not overbake. Cool, then chill thoroughly before loosening edges and removing from pan. Cut into squares. If desired, drizzle melted semisweet chocolate over top. Yields 1 dozen brownies.

The Landmark

601 Second Avenue East
ONEONTA

*K*nown as "the Covered Bridge Capital of Alabama," Blount County boasts three covered bridges, all of which are still in daily use and are marked by road signs on nearby highways. In a couple of hours, you can easily see all three. Perhaps the most picturesque is the Horton Mill Covered Bridge, located north of Oneonta on Alabama 75. This latticed structure looms seventy feet above the Warrior River—higher above running water than any other covered bridge in the country. Each October, the Oneonta area stages its Covered Bridge Festival, which includes bridge tours and arts-and-crafts exhibits.

And while you're seeing the covered bridges of Blount County, stop by The Landmark in Oneonta. As former owner Hal Huie put it, "This place *is* a landmark. It's been here forever."

Actually, *forever* traces back to the 1940s, when an old-fashioned service station occupied the spot—the kind where a crew dashed out to fill your tank, check your tires, and clean your windshield. A restaurant later evolved in conjunction with the gas station. The Melton family ran the business during the 1950s. Then came Jonah's, an eatery noted for its big, whale-shaped sign.

For the past decade, Charlie Bottcher has presided at The Landmark. His clientele comes from a seventy-five-mile radius. A traveler once described his dining experience here as "a little bit of France in the middle of nowhere."

Building his weekly specials around what's fresh, good, and available, Charlie might offer Filet Mignon in Puff Pastry, Spicy Greek Snapper, or Baked Salmon with Pistachio Crumb Crust and Dill Sauce. Chicken Landmark, a signature dish, features a char-broiled, marinated chicken breast topped with crabmeat, char-broiled shrimp, and Clam Sauce. A delicious dish that Charlie calls "Crazy Cajun" features Fried Green Tomatoes and red snapper fillets topped with lightly blackened crawfish and Hollandaise. Charlie shared the secrets of his Spicy Baked Shrimp with Garlic Cheese Grits and his Seafood Puff.

"I've always liked to read cookbooks the way some people read novels," he said, "and I wanted a restaurant of my own forever." Even before that happened, he cooked for fund-raisers and church dinners and occasionally prepared campus brunches for six hundred people during his son's university days. He and his wife, Mary, "always enjoyed entertaining at home," he added. "She did the house and the flower arrangements and I did the cooking."

The Landmark's Crazy Cajun

Beer batter

1 cup Aunt Jemima pancake mix	¾ cup beer

Whip pancake mix and beer together with a whisk. Let stand 30 minutes. Whisk again before using.

Hollandaise

2 cups margarine, cut into pieces	9 egg yolks juice of 1 lemon

Put 1 inch of water in the bottom of a double boiler and turn heat to high. Combine egg yolks, margarine, and lemon juice in top pot; whip continually with a whisk and keep sides of bowl clean with a spatula. When whisk begins to track, transfer sauce to another container. Cover and do not stir until ready to use.

Note: For a small batch, use 5 egg yolks, 1 cup margarine, and juice of ½ lemon.

Seasoned flour

2 cups flour	1 teaspoon pepper
1 teaspoon salt	¾ teaspoon garlic powder

Mix well with a whisk and set aside.

Snapper

6 6-ounce red snapper fillets, skin removed	1 pound crawfish meat, cooked
1 cup butter, melted	4 large green tomatoes, cut into 12 slices
1 small bottle K-Paul's Redfish Seasoning	

Dip fillets in butter, coating both sides; reserve remaining butter. Lightly season one side of each fillet with K-Paul's and reserve remaining seasoning. Char-broil fillets with seasoned side down; cook until just done, approximately 10 minutes per inch of thickness. Remove fillets to platter and keep warm.

Dip tomato slices in beer batter, then coat with seasoned flour. Fry a couple of slices at a time in a deep-fat fryer until golden brown. Remove slices to a platter lined with a paper towel and keep warm.

Place crawfish meat in a saucepan with remaining melted butter. Season lightly with remaining K-Paul's. Heat through, stirring often.

To serve, put two tomato slices in center of each of 6 plates. Place a fillet on top of tomatoes and top each fillet with a spoonful of crawfish meat. Pour Hollandaise over each serving and garnish as desired. Serves 6.

The Landmark's Seafood Puff

1 package Pepperidge Farm
  puff pastry sheets
½ cup butter
1 pound red snapper or
  orange roughy, skin
  removed

5 green onions, white portions
  and ½ of green portions,
  chopped fine
2 tablespoons dry sherry
½ pound lump crabmeat
Hollandaise Sauce (recipe
  above)

Cut 3 fish-shaped pieces in each pastry sheet. Score across fish shapes lightly and cut small oblong hole in center. Place pastry in a lightly greased pan and bake in a 400-degree oven until puffed and golden brown. Remove top of center hole and any dough underneath that is not cooked. Keep puffs warm.

While puff pastry bakes, melt butter in a large saucepan. Add fish, cook until tender, and break into small pieces. Add green onions, stir, and cook 4 to 5 minutes. Add sherry and crabmeat. Stir gently until hot.

Place a thin layer of Hollandaise on each of 6 serving plates and top with a fish-shaped puff pastry. Fill cavity in each pastry with hot fish mixture. Place top over filling. Pour Hollandaise over each pastry, garnish as desired, and serve. Serves 6.

Arman's at ParkLane

2117 Cahaba Road
Mountain Brook
BIRMINGHAM AREA

"*Please* seat me in the produce section."

Staffers at Arman's at ParkLane sometimes hear requests like that, because the restaurant once housed a neighborhood grocery store. Many locals remember the brick structure as ParkLane Market, where they were called by name and the butcher knew exactly

5:00 P.M. until 10:00 P.M.
Monday through Wednesday

5:00 P.M. until 11:00 P.M.
Thursday through Saturday

For reservations (suggested, especially on weekends), call (205) 871-5551.

how they liked their meat cut. The grocery opened in 1921 and served its customers for several decades. Later, the building housed a market specializing in seasonal produce and fresh herbs, and then it stood vacant awhile before its rebirth as an upscale restaurant in Mountain Brook's English Village.

As we entered the restaurant, my husband and I paused to admire the larger-than-life painting of a monk eating noodles, which serves as Arman's logo. To the left of the foyer stands a massive bar of carved mahogany, constructed in 1893 and imported from Chicago. On the wall beyond, hand-painted murals depict the sun-drenched Italian countryside.

An exhibition kitchen fronted by a counter with a row of stools permits patrons to watch the action, which is especially entertaining on busy nights. Other features include a rotisserie and a wood-burning oven, which imparts an oak flavor to the Roasted Fillet of Gulf Red Snapper, the pizzas, and other items.

The handsome, spacious interior features European decor and a serenely monochromatic color scheme — crisp white linens, tones of cream and brown, and narrow-planked oak flooring. We sat at a window table adjacent to the grocery store's original entrance. Arman's also offers patio seating in front, a pleasant option when the weather permits.

Chef Chris Melville, who grows his own fresh herbs and Roma tomatoes behind the restaurant, calls Chef Frank Stitt of Birmingham his mentor. "Frank invited me to assist him with a James Beard food presentation in New York," he said, "and I consider that quite an honor."

When the restaurant opened, the emphasis was on northern Italian cuisine, but it now leans more toward Mediterranean fare. For our appetizers, our server recommended the Seared Diver Boat Scallops and the Wood-Roasted Chicken, which was topped with a portobello mushroom. Both were scrumptious, but the fresh, succulent scallops took top honors.

Among the hearty main courses are such standouts as Grilled Aged Prime Angus Tenderloin of Beef, which comes with a fluffy Sweet Potato Purée and Sautéed Spinach. But it was the Oven-Roasted Monkfish—presented with Bacon-Wrapped Potatoes and Garlic and Sage Cream Sauce—that won my heart.

"Our pastry chef does astonishing things," said Carolyn Bennett, Arman's general manager, "so save room for dessert." We didn't, but in the name of research, my husband and I nonetheless shared an elegant creation called Tiramisu Gâteau, a sponge cake dipped in a coffee-Marsala combination and layered with rich Italian cream cheese and grated chocolate.

Ah, Arman's—I can't wait to return. Next time, I'll sit in the produce section and order a plate of pasta. And I'll attack it with gusto, just like the monk in the painting.

Arman's at ParkLane's Tuscan Tomato and Bread Soup

1 yellow onion, sliced
8 to 10 cloves garlic, peeled
10 to 12 vine-ripened tomatoes, cut into chunks
1 bunch fresh basil, chopped

1 baguette with crust removed, cut into 2-inch pieces (about 8 cups loosely packed)
salt

Combine all ingredients except salt in a large, nonreactive saucepan and simmer gently for 45 minutes. Purée in a Cuisinart or pass through a food mill. Add salt to taste. If desired, garnish with slivers of fresh basil. Serves 4 to 6.

Arman's at ParkLane's Twice-Baked Potatoes

4 large russet potatoes
3 slices bacon
1 cup sour cream
1 tablespoon fresh chives,
    chopped

1½ cups Reggiano
    Parmigiano cheese, grated
salt and pepper to taste

Bake potatoes until done. Cook and crumble bacon and reserve drippings. Cut potatoes in half and scoop contents into a mixing bowl. Combine with sour cream, chives, bacon, drippings, and cheese and season with salt and pepper. Spoon mixture into potato shells and bake 10 to 15 minutes at 350 degrees until golden brown. Serves 8.

Cobb Lane Restaurant

1 Cobb Lane
BIRMINGHAM

$\mathcal{S}$itting under a tree in the courtyard of Cobb Lane Restaurant, I could easily imagine myself at a sidewalk cafe in Paris. Sunlight dappled the white tablecloths and lush greenery and a stone fountain added to the ambiance of this landmark in Birmingham's Five Points South Historic District. Listed on the National Register of Historic Places, the entire area brims with inviting galleries, shops, boutiques, and eateries.

Lunch
11:00 A.M. until 2:30 P.M.
Monday through Saturday

Dinner
5:30 P.M. until 10:30 P.M.
Tuesday through Saturday

For reservations (accepted but not required),
call (205) 933-0462.

Patrons enter Cobb Lane Restaurant through an iron-fenced courtyard via a cobblestone alley just off Twentieth Street between Thirteenth and Fourteenth Avenues South. Depending on the weather, diners can opt for an alfresco meal in a canopy-covered garden setting or eat in one of the cozy rooms tucked away at ground level beneath a turn-of-the-century apartment building. Throughout the restaurant, hand-painted murals depict scenes from the French countryside.

Birmingham natives tend to feel proprietary about this historical eatery, opened by Virginia Cobb in the 1940s as a tearoom called the Corner Cupboard. As a tribute to this businesswoman and her celebrated restaurant, the former Nineteenth Way South address became Cobb Lane during the 1960s. Some of Birmingham's modern-day brides continue to follow a precedent set by their grandmothers and mothers, who chose Cobb Lane as the setting for their bridesmaids' luncheons, rehearsal dinners, and wedding receptions.

Regulars from Cobb Lane's early days still recall the big, furnished dollhouse that once occupied a prominent spot in the courtyard. Although the dollhouse is gone, the charming tradition of children's tea parties continues, says owner Tim Kreider. In fact, his wife, Mandy, had just hosted one before my visit. Dressed in frilly frocks, little girls practice the social graces and enjoy dainty sandwiches as their mothers watch from a discreet distance. The girls depart with memories and keepsake dolls.

When her male clientele began to grow after World War II, Mrs. Cobb supplemented her soups, salads, and sandwiches with more substantial fare, such as Chicken Divan, Chicken Supreme, and Roast Beef. Today's menu still features some of her original recipes.

After dipping into Cobb Lane's famous She-Crab Soup—rich and creamy with a splash of sherry—I selected an entree of Crab Cakes, which were garnished with Rémoulade Sauce and served on a bed of greens. The other options included Tim's hearty specialty sandwiches and a sampler of Chicken, Shrimp, and Tuna Salads. Homemade Butter Rolls accompany each entree.

If you can't resist dessert (and many people fall into that category here), choose the Chocolate Roulage. At Cobb Lane, you can have your roulage and eat it, too, because this light, delicate chocolate cake—swirled jelly-roll fashion with whipped cream—can be purchased as a carry-out.

The restaurant offers a line of recipe books, including *A Stroll Down Cobb Lane: In the Kitchen with a Southern Lady*, compiled by the restaurant's previous owner, Mikki Bond. This delightful book includes recipes passed down from Mrs. Cobb's tenure, plus a collection of Mikki's own culinary creations and humorous anecdotes.

Cobb Lane Restaurant's Crawfish Fritters

3 ears sweet or white corn
1 red bell pepper, diced
½ cup flour
1 tablespoon sugar
1 pinch salt

1 pinch freshly ground pepper
1 pound crawfish, cooked
2 large eggs, beaten lightly
cooking oil

Boil corn for 5 minutes and cut from cob. Combine corn and red pepper in a mixing bowl. Add flour, sugar, salt, pepper, crawfish, and eggs and blend well. Refrigerate for 30 minutes. Pour enough oil into a large skillet to submerge fritters completely and heat to 350 degrees. Drop heaping tablespoons of fritter mixture into heated oil and cook until golden brown. Carefully remove fritters from oil and drain on paper towels. If desired, serve with cocktail or rémoulade sauce and lemon wedges. Serves 4.

Grouper

5-ounce can chipotles in
   adobo sauce
1 tablespoon kosher salt

4 8-ounce fillets fresh
   grouper
Fresh Mango Chutney
   (recipe below)

Combine chipotle peppers, a small amount of adobo sauce, and salt in a food processor and process 2 minutes. Rub fish on all sides with chipotle mixture and refrigerate 2 hours. Oil grill and place fish flesh side down on it. Fish is done when it begins to exude white juice and feels firm to the touch. Serve with Fresh Mango Chutney. Serves 4.

Fresh Mango Chutney

2 fresh mangoes, peeled and
   diced
½ small red onion, diced fine
zest of 1 large lemon
juice of 1 large lemon
zest of 1 lime

1 bunch parsley, chopped
   coarse
2 tablespoons brown sugar
¼ cup champagne vinegar
salt and pepper

Place mangoes and onion in a mixing bowl. Add lemon zest, lemon juice, lime zest, and parsley and mix lightly. Add brown sugar and vinegar and mix to incorporate all ingredients. Add salt and pepper to taste. Refrigerate at least 2 hours before serving.

Note: This is an uncooked version of chutney.

Highlands Bar & Grill

2011 Eleventh Avenue South
BIRMINGHAM

$\mathcal{A}$labama's largest city, Birmingham boasts many exceptional restaurants, but according to a recent *Birmingham News* readers' poll, the best in town is Highlands Bar & Grill. Highlands also captured the "Best Martini" title and shared first-place honors for "Best Bar."

Located in historic Five Points South—the city's colorful soul—the restaurant occupies a tile-topped Spanish Revival building of stucco accented with stone around the door and windows. Built by the Munger family during the late 1920s, the structure served as a tearoom during the late 1930s and early 1940s. Chef Frank Stitt bought the building and opened Highlands in 1982. The Five Points South Historic District was placed on the National Register of Historic Places the following year.

The classically trained Stitt grew up in Cullman, Alabama, the son of a nutritionist and a surgeon. His Southern creations have been dubbed "New American" cuisine. In fact, *Bon Appétit* has called him Alabama's hottest chef, and *Food and Wine* magazine has christened him one of America's "Top 25 New Chefs." Accolades for his cuisine continue to cover walls and fill dining magazines and books. He has received the prestigious James Beard Award as a "Bright Star of American Cooking" and 1996 and 1998 James Beard Foundation nominations for "Best Chef of the Southeast."

Stitt brings his culinary magic to an ever-evolving list of entrees. Celebrated for its Crab Cakes, the restaurant might also serve Grilled Leg of Lamb with Basil Aioli or Pan-Roasted Quail with Corn Pudding. From the tasty Sweet Potato Crostini appetizer to Crawfish Etouffée to Apple Butter Crostata with Rum Raisin Ice Cream, Stitt's innovative twists lift the mundane to exciting heights. Even humble grits get transformed into something glorious here, as evidenced by the Stone-Ground Baked Grits with Wild Mushrooms, Ham, and Thyme. Indeed, Stitt's Cuisine deserves to be written with a capital *C*.

The dining-room atmosphere is relaxed, the bar spirited, and the staff friendly and experienced. All in all, an evening at Highlands Bar

6:00 P.M. until 10:00 P.M.
Tuesday through Thursday

6:00 P.M. until 10:30 P.M.
Friday and Saturday

Bar opens at 4:00 P.M.
Tuesday through Saturday

For reservations (recommended), call (205) 939-1400.

& Grill makes for a dining experience to savor — a taste of Provence in the heart of Dixie.

Highlands Bar & Grill's Crawfish Etouffée

4 tablespoons olive oil
1 onion, chopped fine
2 ribs celery, chopped fine
1 red bell pepper, chopped fine
1 yellow bell pepper, chopped fine
1 carrot, peeled and chopped fine
2 green onions (white and green portions), sliced
2 bay leaves
1 tablespoon fresh thyme, chopped
1 tablespoon fresh basil, chopped
½ teaspoon dried oregano

1 clove garlic, minced
1 shallot, minced
1 pound crawfish meat
½ cup seafood broth, fish stock, shrimp stock, or clam juice
½ cup white wine
1 tomato, seeded and diced
2 tablespoons butter
½ teaspoon cayenne pepper
1 teaspoon paprika
salt and pepper to taste
4 cups cooked rice
chopped parsley, basil, or green onion for garnish

Heat 2 tablespoons olive oil in a large sauté pan. Sauté onion, celery, bell peppers, carrot, and green onions for 5 minutes over medium heat. Add bay leaves, thyme, basil, and oregano and cook another 5 minutes. Remove from pan and set aside. Wipe out pan, heat remaining 2 tablespoons of olive oil, and sauté garlic, shallot, and crawfish about 2 minutes until almost done. Add vegetable mixture, seafood broth, wine, and tomato and cook 2 minutes. Swirl in butter and add cayenne pepper and paprika. Taste and adjust seasonings.

To serve, place rice in center of warm plates and ladle étouffée around it. Garnish with parsley, basil, or green onion. Serves 6 to 8.

Highlands Bar & Grill's Sweet Potato Crostini

8 ½-inch slices baguette or
    sourdough bread
extra-virgin olive oil
2 tablespoons plus 2
    teaspoons fresh goat cheese
2 sweet potatoes, baked and
    sliced

2 red bell peppers, charred,
    with skins and seeds
    removed
pinch of fresh chives, thyme,
    or basil
pinch of sea salt
pinch of freshly ground
    pepper

Rub bread with olive oil and grill or toast lightly. Crumble goat cheese onto bread and top with sweet potato slices. Cut bell peppers into thick strips and place a strip of pepper on top of each potato slice. Anoint with oil and herbs. Serves 8.

Highlands Bar & Grill's Rum Raisin Ice Cream

1½ cups raisins
dark rum
3 cups whole milk
1 vanilla bean

1 cup sugar
9 egg yolks
2 cups heavy cream

Soak raisins in rum overnight. Heat milk and vanilla bean in medium saucepan until steaming. Remove from heat, cover with a plate, and allow milk to steep for 20 to 30 minutes. Whisk sugar and egg yolks together in a large mixing bowl and gradually add hot milk. Split vanilla bean in half lengthwise and scrape seeds into milk mixture; add pod. Pour mixture back into saucepan and cook over medium-low heat, stirring constantly with a wooden spoon until mixture thickly coats spoon. Be careful not to overcook custard, or the eggs will scramble. Remove from heat and pass mixture through a fine sieve into a bowl set in ice water. Stir in cream. Drain raisins and add to ice cream mixture. Stir until mixed. Freeze. Yields about ½ gallon.

The Irondale Cafe

1906 First Avenue North
Irondale
BIRMINGHAM AREA

freight train whistled by as I stopped at The Irondale Cafe, the eatery made famous by Fannie Flagg's novel and the resulting movie, *Fried Green Tomatoes*. The inspiration for the Whistle-Stop Cafe sits beside railroad tracks in the historic section of Irondale. Photos and posters from the movie line the walls of the cafe, where the service is cafeteria-style.

10:45 A.M. until 2:30 P.M.
Sunday through Friday

Call for summer dinner hours.

Reservations are not necessary. For information, call (205) 956-5258.

Collecting a tray, I proceeded past a mouth-watering lineup of Fried Chicken, Pork Chops, Meatloaf, Mashed Potatoes, Black-Eyed Peas, Turnip Greens, Sweet Potatoes, Macaroni and Cheese, and other comfort foods. Each day brings a different selection of meats and a variety of fresh vegetables. But you'll always find that Southern favorite, Fried Green Tomatoes.

"We serve sixty to seventy pounds of green tomatoes a day, and more on Sunday," said Mary Jo McMichael. She and her husband, Billy, own The Irondale Cafe. During the annual Whistle-Stop Day Festival in May, the McMichaels dish up more than two hundred pounds of Fried Green Tomatoes to a triple line of folks filing through.

"When they're cooked just right, they are pretty awesome. If they have even a shimmer of pink, they don't work as well," said Bill Jr., who heads up the family's batter mix division. The breading for the cafe's specialty dish is commercially packaged and available in grocery stores.

The McMichaels bought the cafe on January 1, 1973, from Fannie Flagg's great-aunt Bess, who started the business during the 1930s. The building, which dates to 1926, originally contained thirty-two seats, but an expansion into the adjoining structure has brought the capacity up to about three hundred. "Before we bought a convection oven," said Mrs. McMichael, "we cooked on the same old stove owned by Miss Bess."

Mrs. McMichael, who received the inspiration for most of her recipes by watching her mother, shared her technique for making biscuits. "The secret to good biscuits is to have the mix almost dry," she confided. "I use oil instead of shortening and knead the dough a little bit. Then I roll the dough out and cut the biscuits without turning the cutter."

Because the cafe's recipes have been published in her own *Original Irondale Cafe Whistle-Stop Cookbook* and in Fannie Flagg's cookbook, Mrs. McMichael provided a different version of her recipe for Fried Green Tomatoes—one that uses buttermilk for dipping. The recipe got a thumbs-up signal from the lucky kitchen crew during a sampling session. And my family loved it, too.

Leaving Mrs. McMichael in her office autographing copies of her cookbook for some California visitors who had stopped by for some down-home country cooking, I stepped outside just in time to watch another freight train roll past the Whistle-Stop Cafe.

The Irondale Cafe's Fried Green Tomatoes

5 medium green tomatoes
1 cup self-rising cornmeal
1 cup self-rising flour
⅓ teaspoon salt

¼ teaspoon black pepper
1 cup buttermilk
vegetable oil

Slice tomatoes into ¼-inch slices and set aside. Combine cornmeal, flour, salt, and pepper in a shallow dish. Pour buttermilk into a bowl and add some of the tomatoes, being careful not to stack. Remove slices from bowl and let excess buttermilk drain off. Dip slices into cornmeal mixture. Repeat until all slices are coated. Fry in ½ inch hot oil until brown, turning once to brown other side. Place in a colander to drain. Serve hot. Serves 5 to 6.

The Irondale Cafe's Cracklin' Cornbread

2 cups self-rising cornmeal
2 eggs, beaten
2 cups buttermilk

¼ cup bacon drippings or
vegetable oil
1 cup pork cracklings

Combine cornmeal, eggs, and buttermilk in a mixing bowl and stir until smooth. Heat bacon fat and cracklings in a 9- or 10-inch skillet until almost smoking. Pour batter over hot drippings, cover with lid, and cook over medium heat for about 25 minutes until firm, or bake uncovered in a preheated 425-degree oven for about 25 minutes until firm and golden brown. Serve hot. Serves 8.

Note: Cracklings (crunchy pieces of pork fat after the rendering process, or the crisp brown skin of fried or roasted pork) are sold in specialty markets and in some supermarkets.

Nabeel's Cafe

1706 Oxmoor Road
Homewood
BIRMINGHAM AREA

The Krontiras family—John and Ottavia and their son, Anthony—own and operate Nabeel's Cafe, a neighborhood cafe/deli/bakery/market located in Homewood. The white-painted brick building with green canopies keeps stretching to occupy ever more storefronts. But

9:30 A.M. until 9:30 P.M.
Monday through Saturday

Reservations are not necessary.
For information,
call (205) 879-9292.

even after three expansions, the eatery still manages to evoke an intimate European dining experience.

That the family has succeeded in its goal of offering authenticity and quality can be measured in part by Nabeel's numerous awards, which include being named "Birmingham's Favorite Restaurant" in a recent readers' poll conducted by *Birmingham Magazine*.

"We try to treat customers as if they were guests at our home," said John, who came to the restaurant business after a career as a computer executive.

When the Krontiras family moved here more than two decades ago, Ottavia, originally from northern Italy, started shopping at Nabeel's, a small ethnic grocery store established in 1972 and named for its former Lebanese owner. Ottavia now oversees the market.

During my visit to Nabeel's, I slipped into a high-backed booth and ordered the cafe's celebrated Mint Tea, especially refreshing on a hot August day. John joined me and shared some of the building's history. The structure dates to the early 1940s and once contained a hair salon that served a loyal following for almost five decades. An eatery called Hamburger Heaven, an ice cream shop, a florist, a convenience store, and a music shop have at various times occupied the quarters that now house Nabeel's.

The decor features touches of John's native Greece. He characterizes Nabeel's cuisine as predominantly Mediterranean, though there are several Eastern European dishes on the menu, along with some Russian and Czechoslovakian items.

When I dipped a pita wedge into the Taramasalata Dip, made of red caviar and salted carp roe, I understood why this has become Nabeel's most popular appetizer. John shared the recipe for this delicious spread. He says the cafe and market sell more than 120 pounds of the mixture each week.

From homemade soups and piquant Greek Salad to Stuffed Grape Leaves and sandwich specialties like Fior di Latte (made with fresh mozzarella, roasted peppers, and fresh basil), Nabeel's prepares everything fresh daily. I especially enjoyed the Spanakopita (spinach pie), made of fresh spinach layered with phyllo, feta cheese, and herbs. Ottavia's Chicken Salad gets rave reviews from customers as well. Other favorites include Eggplant Parmesan and a version of Moussaka enhanced by Bechamel Sauce.

Nabeel's divine desserts include Baklava, Cannoli, Butter Cookies, Honey Crescents, and more. Those who can't decide which to try can take home a pastry assortment, as I did.

"One of the unique things about Nabeel's," John pointed out, "is that it's an international market. More than 90 percent of our items you cannot find in a regular grocery store."

The market offers bins of exotic-smelling spices, vats of olives, fifteen kinds of olive oil, beans, nuts, breads, herbs, coffees, teas, bath soaps made from olive oil, and Greek, Italian, Bulgarian, Russian, and Lebanese cheeses. And on your way out, you can pick up a bottle of Nabeel's Classic Greek Dressing, inspired by a recipe from John's father.

Nabeel's Cafe's Taramasalata Dip

6 or 7 slices French or
   Italian bread, crusts
   removed
1 medium white onion,
   chopped fine
8 ounces tarama (a mixture
   of salted mullet or carp roe
   available in specialty and
   gourmet stores)

juice of 2 lemons
1 tablespoon red wine vinegar
1 teaspoon sugar
1 cup extra-virgin olive oil
Kalamata olives
bread or pita wedges

Barely cover bread with water and allow to soak. Squeeze out as much water as possible and allow bread to dry on absorbent paper. Place onion, tarama, lemon juice, vinegar, sugar, and bread in a food processor and process until smooth. With processor running, gradually pour oil through feeder tube. Taste and adjust by adding a little vinegar, oil, or lemon juice; if mixture is salty or smells fishlike, add more lemon juice and oil very slowly. Finished consistency should be something like softly whipped cream, just firm enough to mound slightly when dropped from a spoon. Transfer mixture to a serving bowl and cover tightly. Chill several hours before serving. Garnish with Kalamata olives and serve with crusty bread or pita wedges. Yields approximately 3 cups.

Note: It is best to make this recipe a day ahead to allow time for bread to dry and for flavors to blend.

Nabeel's Cafe's Spanakopita

2 pounds spinach, washed
  thoroughly
1½ cups spring onions,
  chopped
1 cup extra-virgin olive oil
8 ounces feta cheese
4 tablespoons Kefalotyri or
  Parmesan cheese, grated

4 tablespoons parsley,
  chopped
4 sprigs fresh dill, chopped
¾ teaspoon nutmeg
4 eggs, beaten lightly
salt and pepper
12 sheets phyllo dough
melted butter

Trim spinach, removing roots but retaining stems. Shred spinach and place it in a pot of boiling water for 6 to 8 minutes. Drain water and place spinach in a bowl to cool. Sauté onions. Add onions and olive oil to spinach. Stir in cheeses, then add parsley, dill, nutmeg, and eggs. Mix well. Add salt and pepper to taste. Oil a 13- by 9-inch baking pan and line it with 6 sheets of phyllo, brushing each sheet with melted butter. Add 2 inches of spinach filling, spreading evenly. Place remaining 6 sheets of phyllo on top of filling, brushing each sheet with melted butter. Trim phyllo and tuck into sides of pie. Brush top with oil and bake for about 45 minutes in a 375-degree oven. Remove from oven, let cool for 5 minutes, and cut into squares. Serves 6.

The Silvertron Cafe

3813 Clairmont Avenue
BIRMINGHAM

The Silvertron Cafe derives its name from a repair shop that once occupied the premises, where technicians practiced the no-longer-in-demand craft of resilvering picture tubes in early television sets. Owner Alan Potts, who bought the red-brick structure in 1986, says it dates to the late 1920s and saw its first use as a grocery store. A chain supermarket and a hair salon have shared the Clairmont Avenue address also.

Potts worked as a bartender during his college days, which led to a job with a popular chain restaurant. After a decade with the company, including a stint as manager of one of its restaurants, Potts opened The Silvertron in Birmingham's Forest Park. He describes the pleasant, popular neighborhood eatery as a "middle-range restaurant with home-style food."

11:00 A.M. until 10:00 P.M.
Monday through Saturday

11:00 A.M. until 9:00 P.M.
Sunday

Brunch
11:00 A.M. until 2:00 P.M.
Sunday

Reservations are needed only for large groups. For information, call (205) 591-3707.

The cafe's interior features a ceiling of embossed tin, a color scheme of deep rose and gray, black-topped tables, cozy booths, and a virtual gallery of Birmingham's history in the form of framed black-and-white photographs lining the walls.

The Silvertron offers a dizzying array of menu items — salads, pasta, sandwiches, chicken, steaks, seafood, and more. The favorites include Fajitas, Steak Sandwiches, Beef Tenderloin Kabobs, and Chicken Quesadillas. I ordered the Chicken Salad with a side dish of the restaurant's famous Garlic Mashed Potatoes, both of which lived up to their delicious reputation. The Shrimp Salad is frequently requested as well. The Silvertron's Monday Family Pasta Night specials feature a variety of sauces, all freshly made.

The cafe serves scrumptious desserts like Forest Park Pie, made with chocolate chips and pecans. Bailey's Brownie, a show-stopper with French Vanilla Ice Cream, Oreo cookies, whipped cream, and a dram of Irish Mist, is a luscious treat to share with someone over coffee. Thus fortified, you can sally forth to browse the interesting inventory in the Museum Store next door and the bookstore across the street in this inviting neighborhood.

The Silvertron Cafe's Shrimp Salad

6 bay leaves
1 teaspoon cayenne pepper
1 lemon, sliced
2 pounds shrimp, peeled and
  deveined
½ cup mayonnaise

1 bunch green onions,
  chopped
4 ribs celery, chopped
2 teaspoons sea salt
2 teaspoons white pepper

Combine bay leaves, cayenne pepper, and lemon slices in 1½ gallons of water and bring to a boil. Add shrimp and cook about 4 minutes until flesh is opaque. Drain shrimp, place them in a shallow container, and refrigerate. Combine mayonnaise, onions, celery, sea salt, and white pepper. When shrimp are completely cooled, remove lemon slices and toss shrimp with dressing. Refrigerate until ready to use. Serves 6.

The Silvertron Cafe's Olive Salad

⅔ cup green olives, pitted and
  chopped coarse
⅔ cup black olives, pitted and
  chopped coarse
¼ cup pimentos, diced
2 anchovies, mashed
1 tablespoon capers

⅓ cup parsley, chopped fine
1 teaspoon oregano
¼ teaspoon black pepper
½ cup olive oil
3 medium cloves garlic,
  minced

Thoroughly combine all ingredients, chill, and serve. Yields about 1 pint.

The Silvertron Cafe's Garlic Mashed Potatoes

3 large Idaho potatoes, peeled
   and cubed
3 tablespoons butter (no
   substitutes)
½ cup heavy whipping cream
1 tablespoon salt

1 teaspoon cayenne pepper
6 medium cloves garlic,
   peeled and chopped fine
½ cup Parmesan or Romano
   cheese, grated

Bring potatoes to a boil and simmer about 12 minutes until tender.
Drain potatoes and mash lightly with potato masher or heavy fork.
Add butter, cream, salt, pepper, and garlic and mix lightly. Place individual portions in ramekins, top with cheese, and broil until lightly
browned. Serves 4.

The Bright Star

304 Nineteenth Street North
BESSEMER

ounded in 1886 and named in honor of Sir Henry Bessemer, the British engineer who invented the steel-making process, Bessemer soon grew into an important steel-making center. History buffs can get a glimpse of the town's early years at the Bessemer Hall of History Museum, which occupies a 1916 Southern Railroad depot.

11:00 A.M. until 10:00 P.M.
Monday through Saturday

11:00 A.M. until 9:00 P.M.
Sunday

For reservations,
call (205) 424-9444.

Housed in a tall brick building in downtown Bessemer, The Bright Star has played a major role in the town's culinary history. My Birmingham writer friend, Ann, and her husband, Bill, invited me to dine with them at this, their favorite restaurant, more than a decade ago. Since that first visit, I have returned several times and added The Bright Star to my own list of favorites.

At this landmark eatery, brothers Jimmy and Nicky Koikos carry on a family culinary tradition that started in 1907. From its beginnings as a small cafe with a horseshoe-shaped bar, the eatery outgrew three locations before moving to its present site in 1915. It was here that patrons were introduced to The Bright Star's mirrored and marbled walls and ceiling fans. The restaurant's attractive interior features roomy glass-topped booths and murals dating from 1915, painted by a European artist who was traveling through the area.

A Silver Spoon Award recipient, The Bright Star offers an extensive menu with Greek flair. The daily luncheon specials include Beef Tenderloin Tips, Trout Amandine, and Broiled Chicken Greek-Style. The side-dish choices include such items as Fried Eggplant, Corn on the Cob, Creamed Potatoes, Candied Yams, and Pickled Beets. All salad dressings are made fresh daily, and all food is prepared per table order. The seafood dishes feature fresh fish straight from the gulf coast. The Bright Star's signature dishes — Broiled Snapper and Beef Tenderloin Greek-Style — have been attracting patrons for generations.

My most recent dinner started with a cup of savory Seafood Gumbo, followed by a zesty Greek Salad. As my main course, I chose the Beef Tenderloin Greek-Style, though I was also tempted by the Lobster and Crabmeat au Gratin, the Broiled Seafood Platter, and the Blackened Snapper, which is prepared New Orleans–style. When it came time to top off my meal, I chose from a variety of fresh, homemade pies—Chocolate Almond, Peanut Butter, Pineapple Cheese, Banana Nut, Coconut Cream, and Lemon Icebox.

On Friday and Saturday evenings, the restaurant features Commanders' Palace Bread Pudding, topped with homemade Whiskey Sauce, and Bananas Foster Short Cake.

The Bright Star's Spinach and Rice Casserole

1 cup butter
½ cup flour
4 cups milk
3 eggs
2 pounds spinach, cooked and
   chopped

½ cup cooked rice
2 cups feta cheese, crumbled
¼ cup green onions, chopped
salt and white pepper to taste
¼ cup Parmesan cheese
1 tablespoon paprika

Melt butter, add flour, and stir until thoroughly mixed. Cook about 2 minutes, then allow to cool slightly. Place milk in a large saucepan and heat to simmering. Add flour mixture a little at a time. Whip to break up lumps, then whip in eggs until creamy and smooth. Let simmer 10 to 15 minutes. Place spinach in the bottom of a 3-quart casserole and add rice, feta cheese, and green onions. Add salt and white pepper. Pour cream sauce over top and sprinkle with Parmesan and paprika. Bake at 350 degrees for 20 to 25 minutes. Serves 10 to 12.

The Bright Star's Red Snapper Greek-Style

½ cup cooking oil
6 7-ounce snapper fillets
2 cups flour

1½ cups olive oil
juice of 2 to 3 lemons
2 tablespoons oregano

Heat cooking oil in a large skillet. Dredge fillets in flour and place in skillet. Brown fillets on each side about 4 minutes. Combine olive oil and lemon juice, then add oregano. Place fish on plates, ladle about 2 ounces of olive oil mixture over top, and serve. Serves 6.

2 cups olive oil
½ cup plus 1 tablespoon
  lemon juice
2 tablespoons garlic, minced
2 teaspoons oregano

salt and pepper to taste
¾ cup butter
4 10-ounce tenderloins,
  cleaned and butterflied

Combine olive oil, ½ cup lemon juice, 1½ tablespoons garlic, 1 tea-spoon oregano, and salt and pepper. Place tenderloins in marinade for 2 to 3 hours. Melt butter and add remaining garlic, lemon juice, and oregano; mix thoroughly. Broil or char-broil tenderloins to de-sired doneness. Transfer to plates and top with butter sauce. Serves 4.

Barrett's Brewpub & Eatery

2325 University Boulevard
TUSCALOOSA

ℋoused in an Art Deco brick building embellished with glass blocks, Barrett's Brewpub & Eatery stands on what a 1926 publication called Tuscaloosa's "most valuable corner." This junction has also been the site of a hotel and the county jail.

Barrett's occupies the former Brown's Department Store building, encompassing three stories plus a basement. In 1898, Abe Brown founded Brown's Dollar Store, forerunner of the department store. He moved his operation to this cor-

Brewpub
11:00 A.M. until midnight
Monday through Saturday

Upstairs at Barrett's
6:00 P.M. until 11:00 P.M.
Wednesday through Saturday

Buffet
10:00 A.M. until 2:00 P.M.
Sunday

For reservations (strongly recommended for Upstairs at Barrett's), call (205) 366-0380.

ner in 1906, occupying a building that had formerly housed a saloon, with billiard tables in the rooms above. During the eight decades of the Brown family's tenure, the store thrived and underwent a couple of major renovations. A 1940 transformation gave it its current look. The store closed in 1978, and family descendants later donated the building to the local Heritage Commission. For many years, the venerable structure stood vacant.

It was John Barrett Moss and Bob High who came up with the idea of a restaurant reincarnation. Once the passage of the Alabama Brewpub Act of 1992 paved the road for the preservation and alternative use of this historic structure (and others in the state), the partners established a brewpub and restaurant.

The handsome wooden-floored building now houses gleaming stainless-steel brewing equipment, positioned on a level just above the circular bar. Barrett's Spoonbill Porter took first place and its Blonde third place for beers in a Florida competition. These and other housebrewed beers complement a varied menu that includes pizzas, pasta, sandwiches, ribs, steaks, seafood, and more.

Lunch in the brewpub might start with a bowl of delicious Cheese Soup, made with beer and sausage, followed by Cajun Shrimp Pasta, a

Cajun Chicken Pizza (with black beans, cilantro, and jack cheese), or a Salmon Piccata Pizza (with capers and asiago cheese).

In the portion of the operation known as "Upstairs at Barrett's," you can indulge in fine fare—and perhaps pick up a few culinary tips from watching Armand DeLorenz create his masterpieces in the exhibition kitchen. Formerly affiliated with Arman's at ParkLane in Birmingham, he is an internationally known chef who has prepared his renowned specialties for London's Savoy patrons and served as executive chef on the luxury liner *Queen Elizabeth II*.

You might find Deep-Fried Asparagus with Citrus Vinaigrette, Lobster Hash, Stuffed Breast of Chicken (served with Peach and Pecan Chutney), and the luscious New Mexican Bread Pudding on the menu. But if not, whatever is featured during your visit is sure to be equally stellar.

Barrett's Brewpub & Eatery's Stuffed Breast of Chicken

1 cup mozzarella, grated
2 tablespoons extra-virgin
  olive oil
2 cloves garlic, minced
kosher salt and ground black
  pepper to taste

4 boneless chicken breasts
  with skin
8 fresh basil leaves
1 tablespoon butter
Peach and Pecan Chutney
  (recipe below)

Combine mozzarella, 1 tablespoon olive oil, garlic, and salt and pepper and set aside. Slit a pocket into the thickest part of each chicken breast. Place ¼ of the stuffing and 2 basil leaves in each pocket. Close pockets with toothpicks. Heat remaining tablespoon of olive oil and butter in skillet over medium-high heat. Sauté chicken about 7 minutes with skin side down. Turn and sauté 5 minutes more or until done. Remove and place on top of Peach and Pecan Chutney. Serves 4.

Peach and Pecan Chutney

½ cup unfiltered cider
4 tablespoons honey
2 tablespoons pickled ginger,
  minced
pinch of kosher salt
juice of 1 lemon

juice of 2 limes
4 ripe peaches, unpeeled
1 tablespoon jalapeño
  peppers, seeded and minced
½ cup pecan halves, toasted
  slightly

Combine cider, honey, ginger, salt, lemon juice, and lime juice in a skillet and cook over moderate heat for 5 to 6 minutes. Stir in peaches and cook over low heat for 6 to 7 minutes until soft but not mushy. Remove from heat, cool slightly, and slip skin off peaches. Chop peaches and return to skillet. Stir in jalapeños and pecans. Cool to room temperature. Yields 2 to 3 cups.

Barrett's Brewpub & Eatery's New Mexican Bread Pudding

10 cups day-old French
  bread, cut into bite-size
  pieces
¾ cup raisins
½ cup Madeira
2 cups granulated sugar
3½ cups water
5 tablespoons unsalted butter

1½ teaspoons canella or
  regular cinnamon
1½ teaspoons vanilla
juice of 1 lemon
1 cup Monterey Jack or
  cheddar cheese, shredded
1 pint whipping cream,
  whipped to soft peaks

Heat oven to 350 degrees. Place bread in a 9- by 13-inch baking dish and toast until golden. Place raisins in a bowl, cover with Madeira, and soak for 20 minutes. Drain, reserving raisins and Madeira separately. Place sugar in a heavy skillet over medium heat and cook until fully melted and golden in color. Add water; stand well back, as mixture will spatter. Mixture will then solidify; reheat until it returns to a liquid. Reduce heat to low. Add butter, cinnamon, vanilla, and lemon juice. Sprinkle raisins over bread, then pour Madeira and sugar syrup over bread and sprinkle with grated cheese. Bake 20 minutes at 350 degrees. Serve in individual bowls with dollops of whipped cream. Serves 10.

Mezzanine

508 Greensboro Avenue
TUSCALOOSA

"Wow, that's great!" With every menu item, the staff at Mezzanine works to elicit that response from patrons.

"I wanted to provide the kind of cuisine you could find in the finest European restaurants," said Dr. Eugene Mangieri, who owns the establishment. "What I envisioned was a restaurant to provide a different-enough niche—an elegant restaurant with reasonable prices, similar to what you might find in New Orleans or Europe."

Toward that end, the restaurant

Lunch
11:00 A.M. until 2:00 P.M.
Monday through Saturday

Dinner
5:30 P.M. until 10:00 P.M.
Monday through Thursday

5:30 P.M. until 11:00 P.M.
Friday and Saturday

For reservations (recommended),
call (205) 752-0020.

combines careful preparation with the finest fresh products available— aged cheese from caverns in France, beef from a Texas ranch, and truffles, that prized fungus sniffed out by trained dogs.

According to local historians, the structure that houses Mezzanine dates back to 1920 and is a former mercantile store. Today, revolving tie racks and expressionless mannequins have given way to French-made chairs and large urns with striking floral arrangements. Mezzanine's interior projects a timeless quality and a relaxed European feeling. Romantic lighting enhances both the main dining area and the mezzanine level. On the second floor, you'll find jazz and the Cigar Bar, where an exhibit of black-and-white photos depicts the Cuban landscape and its people. Also on the premises is a state-of-the-art kitchen complete with a copper-hooded stove and a wood-burning oven.

Executive Chef Anthony Kirkman, originally from Seattle, describes his cuisine this way: "France meets the South." At lunch, you might find wood-fired pizzas, the Cornmeal-Encrusted Grouper Sandwich (served on a caramelized onion bun with Caper Rémoulade), and Lobster, Goat Cheese, and Fried Green Tomato Salad with Tabasco Vinaigrette.

Dinner might start with an appetizer of Carpaccio of Beef with Horseradish Vinaigrette, then move on to Angel Hair Pasta with Lobster-Shrimp Ragout. Other favorites include Pan-Seared Veal Loin, Lamb

Loin with Creamy Fontina Polenta, and Grilled Prime Beef Tenderloin, served with Goat Cheese–Horseradish Mashed Potatoes and Braised Wild Mushrooms.

Crème Brûlée ranks as the favorite sweet ending. Or you might try something like White Chocolate Macadamia Nut Bread Pudding with Mango Ice Cream and Rum Glaze. Everything here is superb—including the attentive but unobtrusive service.

The last line on Mezzanine's dinner menu reads, "Karma me, Karma you. Have fun, Eat well, and Love someone."

Mezzanine's Granny Smith Apple Vinaigrette

½ cup apple cider vinegar
1 teaspoon garlic, minced
1 teaspoon shallots, diced fine
1 cup extra-virgin olive oil
½ cup hazelnut oil

2 Granny Smith apples,
    peeled, cored, and diced fine
Tupelo honey to taste
1 sprig fresh mint, shredded
salt and freshly ground black
    pepper to taste

Combine vinegar, garlic, and shallots in a mixing bowl. Slowly whisk in oils, then add apples, honey, mint, and salt and pepper. Yields about 2½ cups.

Note: This is an unemulsified vinaigrette and will separate. It is best if prepared a day in advance so flavors can marry.

Mezzanine's Crawfish-Andouille Grits

6 ounces andouille sausage,
    diced
4 ribs celery, diced fine
1 large Texas sweet or
    Vidalia onion, diced fine
1 teaspoon shallots, diced fine
1 teaspoon garlic, minced
2 cups lobster stock
2 cups tomato stock

2 cups heavy cream
2 cups stone-ground grits
8 ounces crawfish meat,
    cleaned
fresh basil, thyme, and
    oregano to taste
salt and pepper to taste
½ cup unsalted butter

Render sausage with celery, onion, shallots, and garlic in a large saucepan. Sweat the vegetables and deglaze with lobster stock. Add tomato stock and heavy cream. Bring to a boil, slowly stir in grits, and cook until almost done. Add crawfish, herbs, and salt and pepper. Add butter and stir until melted. Serves 10 to 12.

Mezzanine's Saffron-Lobster Risotto

2 tablespoons extra-virgin
    olive oil
1 medium carrot, diced fine
4 ribs celery, diced fine
1 yellow onion, diced fine
1 teaspoon garlic, minced
2 cups Arborio rice, uncooked

4 cups lobster stock
saffron to taste
½ cup Parmesan cheese,
    grated
1 bunch fresh basil, shredded
salt and pepper to taste
1 cup lobster meat

Heat olive oil in a large skillet. Add carrot, celery, onion, and garlic and sweat until translucent. Add rice and sauté until lightly coated with oil. Add lobster stock in 3 equal portions, waiting until rice has absorbed all of previous portion; add saffron with first portion. Add cheese, basil, and salt and pepper and cook until al dente. Add lobster and serve. Serves 8 to 10.

The Globe

430 Main Avenue
NORTHPORT

"hou'rt a scholar; let us therefore eat and drink."

This bit of Shakespearean dialogue might have been spoken by Jeff Wilson or Gary Wise, two actors who met during a university production of *Richard II*. After their college days, they decided to launch a restaurant in the old Adams Drug Store building in Northport, a town settled about 1813 just across the Black Warrior River from Tuscaloosa.

As for the restaurant's name, the partners settled on The Globe. Shakespeare used it for his theater, and back in the 1820s and 1830s, Northport boasted a hotel of the same name only a short stroll from where the restaurant now stands. Also, the owners wanted a name that would suggest their menu's international focus.

The Globe opened in August 1993 with Jeff as chef and Gary greeting the public and handling management and bookkeeping. Appreciative audiences kept the partners so busy that they found it necessary to enlarge the restaurant, which they accomplished by knocking a hole through the wall to the adjoining structure, a former dry-goods store. An archway permits easy passage between the two structures, both of which were built in 1909.

Some people claim The Globe has a ghost. When someone is there alone, how else can the sounds of footsteps and doors opening and closing be explained? Or the apparition that bears an uncanny resemblance to the overalls-clad man with a white mustache and white hair depicted in an old photograph found in the building?

Spotlighting the Bard, the decor features framed reproductions of woodcuts from the *First Folio*. Drawings of Shakespearean characters share billing with photos of downtown Northport in earlier years. The Globe's walls also showcase the work of local artists.

Recently, Gary sold his interest in the business to Jeff and his wife, Kathy. Although The Globe keeps them busy, Jeff and Kathy still find time to do an occasional play. When I visited, they had just finished performing in *A Streetcar Named Desire*.

Lunch
11:00 A.M. until 3:00 P.M.
Tuesday through Saturday

Dinner
5:00 P.M. until 10:00 P.M.
Tuesday through Thursday

5:00 P.M. until 11:00 P.M.
Friday and Saturday

For information,
call (205) 391-0949.

A writer friend from the University of Alabama joined me at The Globe for lunch, and we both ordered the Athenian Pasta Salad. Another popular lunch item is The Globe's Quesadillas, which come in a vegetarian version or with grilled chicken, shrimp, Creole crawfish, or jumbo lump crabmeat.

Dinner appetizers include Baked Brie, Olive Pâté, and Indian Samosas, which are puff pastries filled with a vegetable-spice mixture and accompanied by Blueberry Chutney. Among the favorite entrees is Thai Emerald Curry, which features jumbo black tiger shrimp paired with Jasmine Rice. The menu's global influence manifests itself in such items as Caribbean Island Stew, Scallops Madrid, and Jamaican Jerk Chicken.

A fitting finale is the celebrated Chocolate Espresso Cheesecake. To borrow from Katharina in *The Taming of the Shrew*, this delectable dessert is "a dish that I do love to feed upon." And so might you, because Jeff shared the recipe.

The Globe's Chocolate Espresso Cheesecake

9-ounce package Famous chocolate wafers
6 tablespoons butter, melted
1 tablespoon confectioners' sugar
2 tablespoons espresso powder
1 tablespoon water
3 8-ounce packages cream cheese, softened
1 cup sugar
3 eggs
¼ cup butter, melted
1 tablespoon coffee, ground fine
6 ounces bittersweet chocolate
¼ cup heavy cream

Combine chocolate wafers, 6 tablespoons melted butter, and confectioners' sugar in a food processor and pulse until fine. Press mixture into the bottom of a 9-inch springform pan. Wipe out processor bowl and add espresso powder, water, cream cheese, sugar, eggs, ¼ cup melted butter, and coffee and process until very smooth. Pour over crust. Melt chocolate in a saucepan over low heat, then whisk in cream a little at a time. Place 5 dollops of chocolate mixture on top of cream cheese mixture and swirl with a knife. Bake at 350 degrees about 50 minutes until done. Center should remain soft; cake will appear underdone but will firm up. Remove from oven and let stand until cake reaches room temperature, then refrigerate overnight. Serves 10 to 12.

The Globe's House Dressing

1 cup fresh basil
5 cloves garlic
1 cup Parmesan cheese, grated

1 cup extra-virgin olive oil
½ teaspoon black pepper
1 cup rice vinegar

Place basil, garlic, cheese, olive oil, and pepper in a food processor and blend until chopped fine. Pour into a bowl, add rice vinegar, and whisk until blended. Yields about 3 cups.

The Globe's Corn and Wild Rice Soup

4 quarts chicken stock
¾ cup uncooked wild rice
3 cups whole corn
¾ cup kielbasa, diced
2 carrots, peeled and diced

2 medium sweet onions, diced
1 tablespoon butter
1 cup half-and-half
fresh parsley or chives, chopped

Bring 2 quarts of stock to a simmer in a heavy, medium-sized saucepan over medium heat. Add rice and simmer until all liquid evaporates. Stir in half the corn and a cup of stock and cook until thick. Sauté sausage and vegetables in butter in a skillet until onions are translucent, then add to rice. Stir in remaining corn, chicken stock, and cream and cook to desired consistency. Garnish with parsley or chives. Serves 8 to 10.

Ca-John's Faunsdale Bar & Grill

Main Street
FAUNSDALE

ℰach spring, thousands of folks flock to Faunsdale (population ninety-eight) for the Alabama Crawfish Festival with its live entertainment — and for Ca-John's cooking as well.

"In true Cajun cooking, you take what you've got and make it taste good," said John "Ca-John" Broussard, "and you don't waste any of it." As a youngster growing up in southern Louisiana, Ca-John caught crawfish in the swamplands. Now, he raises his own on a nearby farm.

11:00 A.M. until 11:00 P.M.
Saturday

Lunch
11:00 A.M. until 2:00 P.M.
Monday through Friday

Dinner
5:00 P.M. until 9:00 P.M.
Wednesday and Thursday

5:00 P.M. until 10:00 P.M.
Friday

For reservations, call (334) 628-3240.

Faunsdale, located just east of Demopolis, is home to Ca-John's Faunsdale Bar & Grill, housed in a 1905 mercantile building on the town's main street. During the 1950s and 1960s, a cotton warehouse and a seed-cleaning operation occupied the premises. The rambling restaurant has since spilled over into adjacent structures. A pirogue, a pot-bellied stove, a fireplace, and a wall of cattle brands add to the ambiance. The grill opened about a decade ago. Ca-John, after making Faunsdale a crawfish mecca, bought it from the previous owner.

Ca-John's serves great steaks and seafood and a variety of crawfish specialties in season—from Etouffée to Crawfish Pie to Crawfish Pistolettes (French rolls filled with a spicy mixture of crawfish tails, cheese, onions, celery, bell pepper, and jalapeños). The food attracts diners from distant towns. Every Saturday night, patrons can enjoy live entertainment along with the crawfish and other tasty dishes.

Because Louisianans love festivals, most any topic will do for a celebration—especially crawfish. So, in the spring of 1992, when Ca-John could not make his annual pilgrimage to take in Louisiana's festivities, he launched the Alabama Crawfish Festival. Some three thousand people attended that first festival—and ate fifteen hundred pounds of crawfish. Each year since, the festival has grown. Last April, about forty-five thousand people descended on Faunsdale, consumed twenty-two thousand pounds of crawfish, and listened to everything from Cajun and country music to blues, jazz, swamp rock, pop, and zydeco.

Although he doesn't usually share his recipes, Ca-John sat at my table and jotted down some of his favorites.

"Do you use a sauce on your Bread Pudding?" I asked.

"Faunsdale is not that kind of place," he said. "We like to keep things simple here."

Follow the recipes below to try Ca-John's Jambalaya, Crawfish Pie, and Bread Pudding, and let the good times roll. Or, as they say in Cajun country, "Laissez les bon temps rouler!"

Ca-John's Faunsdale Bar & Grill's Jambalaya

1 pound smoked pork sausage links
2 medium onions, chopped
3 cups water

salt, pepper, or other seasonings to taste
3 cups uncooked instant rice

Cut sausage links into ¼-inch slices and fry in a heavy roaster. Remove sausage and sauté onions in sausage drippings. Add water and seasonings. Bring to a boil, then add sausage and rice. Let steam for 5 minutes. Allow mixture to sit 20 minutes before serving. Serves 8.

Ca-John's Faunsdale Bar & Grill's Crawfish Pie

¼ cup margarine
3 medium onions, chopped
1 bell pepper, chopped
1 rib celery, chopped
1 pound crawfish tail meat

1 can cream of mushroom soup
12-ounce can evaporated milk
2 pie shells and top crusts

Melt margarine in a skillet. Add onions, bell pepper, and celery and sauté until onions are translucent. Sauté crawfish in a separate pan. Combine vegetables, crawfish, soup, and evaporated milk and place in pie shells. Cover with top crusts, pinching edges to seal. Cut slits in top crusts and bake in a 350-degree oven for about 1 hour. Yields 2 pies.

Ca-John's Faunsdale Bar & Grill's Bread Pudding

8 cups stale French bread,
   broken into bite-size pieces
3 eggs, beaten

¼ cup sugar
2 cups milk
1 teaspoon vanilla

Place bread in a 9- by 13-inch baking dish. Combine remaining ingredients and pour over bread. Bake at 350 degrees for 30 minutes.

Note: If bread is fresh, it will not absorb flavors. Leave loaf unwrapped for half a day before using.

Major Grumbles

1300 Water Avenue
SELMA

$\mathcal{W}$hile exploring Selma's downtown historic district and waterfront, my husband and I sauntered into Major Grumbles, a gourmet pub on the bank of the Alabama River. Named for a colorful character from Selma's history, the restaurant occupies a brick structure

11:00 A.M. until 11:00 P.M.
Monday through Saturday

Reservations are needed only for groups of six or more. For information, call (334) 872-2006.

built as a cotton warehouse in the 1830s. During the Civil War, when Selma served as a major munitions depot, the building housed a large labor force that produced weaponry and clothing for the Confederate cause. Subsequent enterprises headquartered here included a wholesale grocery and a marine outfitter and distributor, according to Gary Frederickson, who left an aviation career to take on the culinary duties at Major Grumbles.

Gary and his wife, Misti, bought the restaurant from her parents, Martha and Howard Strickland, who had established Major Grumbles more than a decade earlier with the idea of slowing down. Instead, they found that the eatery's appreciative clientele kept them busier than ever.

As we entered, we passed the restaurant's two original black iron gates—said to be slave doors—which weigh about four hundred pounds each. We also saw Mortimer (a regular here) seated on a Confederate flag atop a short flight of stairs. Misti assured us that this century-old skeleton did not meet his fate by starvation at Major Grumbles. In fact, so generous are the restaurant's portions that my husband and I shared the famed Flounder Sandwich, made with thick slices of homemade bread—perfect with a cup of soup. Carlton chose the cheese-topped Potato Soup, and I opted for the mouth-watering Red Bean and Rice Soup.

Some patrons claim that Major Grumbles serves the best Reuben Sandwich on the planet. This grilled creation comes with Fries and homemade Coleslaw laced with dill for added zest. Everything here— including the sauces, the bread for sandwiches, the salad dressings, and the desserts—is created from scratch.

Martha Strickland developed the restaurant's justly famous Marinated Chicken Breast Sandwich, a char-broiled specialty. This heart-healthy dish made with fresh herbs remains one of the restaurant's signature items. Served with pasta, the Marinated Chicken Breast is a popular dinner choice, too. "We try to be health-conscious and fry very little here," said Misti. "Most of our foods are baked or grilled."

Other dinner entrees include Baked Shrimp stuffed with Crabmeat Dressing and a variety of steaks, including the oft-requested Filet Mignon. For those who prefer a light evening meal, lunch selections are available throughout the day.

The homemade Cheesecake with Strawberry and Amaretto Topping makes a perfect sweet finish to a Major Grumbles feast.

Major Grumbles's Stuffed Mushrooms

8 large mushrooms
½ cup extra-virgin olive oil
½ cup butter
1 tablespoon chives, chopped
⅛ teaspoon ground mustard

½ cup dry white wine
8 ounces lump crabmeat
4 slices jalapeño jack cheese
16 shrimp (36-42 count),
*   peeled and cooked*

Remove stems from mushroom caps; chop stems and set aside. Place caps hollow side up in a 9- by 9-inch pan in 2 groups of 4. Combine olive oil, butter, chives, mustard, wine, crabmeat, and chopped stems in a medium-size saucepan and simmer 2 to 3 minutes. Put about 1 ounce of crabmeat mixture in each mushroom cap, then cover each group of 4 with a slice of cheese. Place 2 shrimp on top of cheese over each cap, then place second slice of cheese over that. Pour remaining sauces from pan over top and bake in a 350-degree oven until cheese melts. Serve hot over lettuce leaves, if desired. Serves 4.

Major Grumbles's Red Bean and Rice Soup

1 teaspoon garlic salt
1 teaspoon cayenne pepper
1 teaspoon salt
1 teaspoon black pepper
1 teaspoon white pepper
1½ teaspoons chili powder
3 teaspoons paprika
¾ pound Hillshire Farms
   smoked sausage
⅓ cup margarine

1 medium green pepper,
   chopped
1 medium white onion,
   chopped
3 16-ounce cans dark red
   kidney beans, undrained
3 cups water
3 15-ounce cans tomato
   sauce
¾ cup uncooked instant rice

Combine spices in a small container. Split sausage lengthwise and cut into ⅛- to ¼-inch slices. Melt margarine in a large pot over medium heat. Add green pepper, onion, sausage, and half of spice mixture. Sauté until vegetables are soft, then add kidney beans, water, and tomato sauce. Bring to a boil and taste for flavor; if desired, add more spice mixture. Turn off heat but leave pot on burner. Add rice and mix well. Cover and let sit for 10 minutes. Serve hot. Serves 10 to 12.

Major Grumbles's Shrimp Etouffée

¼ cup vegetable oil
1 large onion, chopped coarse
1 small green bell pepper,
   chopped coarse
2 medium celery ribs,
   chopped coarse
1½ pounds shrimp (36-42
   count), peeled and deveined
1 teaspoon salt

¼ teaspoon cayenne pepper
2 tablespoons flour
1½ cups water
1 tablespoon Panola
   Gourmet Pepper Sauce or
   other hot sauce
1 tablespoon parsley, minced
4½ cups cooked rice

Heat oil in a large skillet over medium-high heat. Sauté onion until slightly soft. Add bell pepper and celery and sauté 5 minutes. Add shrimp, salt, and cayenne pepper and cook no more than 3 minutes, stirring frequently. Sprinkle flour over contents and stir well. Add water and bring to a boil. Reduce heat and simmer for 2 minutes. Stir in hot sauce and sprinkle with parsley. Serve over rice. Serves 6 to 8.

Tally-Ho Restaurant

507 Mangum Avenue
SELMA

*T*all cedar trees flank the entrance to Tally-Ho Restaurant, and a friendly ambiance awaits within. Situated just off Summerfield Road in the northern section of Selma, Tally-Ho stands right in the middle of a residential area. But it arrived first—before the neighbor-

Dinner
5:00 P.M. until 10:00 P.M.
Monday through Saturday

For reservations (recommended), call (334) 872-1390.

hood. A restaurant since 1942, Tally-Ho evolved from a private cabin made of cedar logs. At various times, the premises have been occupied by a hunt club, stables, a driving range, and an off-base officers' club—in fact, squadron names are still visible on the ceiling in the lounge area.

When Bob Kelley bought the place in 1980, he opened the previously private club to the public for dinner. His menu explains the eatery's name: "It was the custom for kings of merrie olde England to entertain guests with a fox hunt. The rider who saw the fox first would cry out Tally Ho and he would lead the chase. Soon the drivers of public coaches would cry out Tally Ho." The cry thus came to symbolize *first* or *best*—and *best* certainly describes Bob's cuisine.

Having spent his boyhood in Europe, Bob developed an appreciation for French cuisine and its sauces early on. Today, his Seafood Casserole is such a favorite that when he makes it, the staff uses a phone request list to notify patrons.

My server recommended an appetizer of Oysters Royale, topped with Parmesan cheese, sour cream, and green onions. When the oysters disappeared, she suggested dipping my homemade bread in the remaining sauce. The Crab Claws, another popular appetizer, come fried or sautéed. Menu items are enhanced by rosemary, thyme, basil, parsley, sage, mint, and other herbs grown on the restaurant's grounds.

The entrees run the gamut from seafood and chicken dishes to London Broil, Prime Rib, and Grilled Pork Chops with Rosemary Sauce, and all come with moist, delicious Zucchini Muffins and a choice of Baked Potato, Steak Fries, Fettuccine, or Seasoned Rice. My Chicken and Shrimp Sauté, topped with almonds, was delectable. And the one you make at home can be, too, because Bob shared the recipe.

When you visit Tally-Ho, be sure to save room for the Amaretto Soufflé or the Chocolate Cheesecake.

"We treat people like family," said Bob, who's been known to dance a jig on the table at a customer's request.

Tally-Ho Restaurant's Society Shrimp

¼ cup butter
1 bunch green onions,
   chopped
1 tablespoon crystallized
   ginger, chopped
1 pound shrimp (21-25
   count), peeled and deveined

2 teaspoons sesame seeds,
   toasted
1 teaspoon poppy seeds
½ teaspoon celery seeds
2 tablespoons soy sauce
toast points

Melt butter in a sauté pan. Add onions and ginger and sauté for 3 minutes. Add shrimp. Stir until shrimp turn pink, then add seeds and soy sauce. Stir another minute until shrimp are covered with seeds. Serve on toast points. Serves 6 to 8.

Tally-Ho Restaurant's Curry-Crab Soup

¾ pound lump crabmeat
¼ cup butter
1½ tablespoons flour
1 cup milk
4 cups half-and-half
½ teaspoon curry powder

1 tablespoon dry sherry
pinch of cayenne pepper
salt and pepper to taste
fresh parsley or chives,
   chopped

Clean crabmeat and set aside. Melt butter, stir in flour, and cook until smooth. Slowly stir in milk and let bubble about 10 minutes; do not boil. Stir in half-and-half, crabmeat, curry powder, and sherry. Add cayenne pepper and salt and pepper, stirring constantly. Bring to serving temperature. Pour into warmed bowls and garnish with parsley or chives. Serves 6.

Tally-Ho Restaurant's Chicken and Shrimp Sauté

¼ cup butter
½ cup green pepper, diced
1 medium onion, julienned
1½ pounds chicken breast,
   cut into bite-size pieces
12 ounces shrimp (90-110
   count), peeled

20 small mushrooms,
   quartered
3 ounces dry sherry
2 tablespoons Worcestershire
   sauce
3 cups cooked rice
½ cup sliced almonds,
   sautéed in butter

Melt butter and sauté pepper and onion about 1 minute in a heavy skillet. Remove vegetables, add chicken to skillet, and sauté until cooked. Add shrimp, mushrooms, pepper, and onion. When shrimp are pink, add sherry and Worcestershire sauce. Serve over rice; pour pan juices on top and sprinkle with almonds. Serves 4 to 6.

Troup House Restaurant

St. James Hotel
1200 Water Avenue
SELMA

The St. James Hotel evokes a flavor of Selma's Old South, cotton-rich, aristocratic past. Positioned on a bluff above the Alabama River, the 1837 hotel provided lodging for both steamboat passengers who stepped ashore at the city docks and travelers arriving at the nearby railroad station.

First opened as the Brantley Hotel, the property became the St. James in 1871. During a recent renovation, an excavation uncovered artifacts dating from 1838 to around 1893. A glass case in the hallway contains memorabilia from this early period: a clay smoking pipe, a doorknob, porcelain marbles, an English plate, embossed patent medicine bottles, oyster shells, a quarter minted in 1873, and an original Troup House menu.

Breakfast
6:00 A.M. until 10:00 A.M.
Daily

Lunch
11:00 A.M. until 2:00 P.M.
Daily

Dinner
5:30 P.M. until 9:00 P.M.
Monday through Thursday

5:30 P.M. until 10:00 P.M.
Friday and Saturday

Sunday dinner is served in the bar.

For reservations (required for dinner), call (334) 872-3234.

The newly restored, camel-colored hotel features elegant rooms and suites and a ballroom overlooking a central courtyard with a fountain. Furnished with antique pieces, the lobby exudes a welcoming ambiance, as does the Drinking Room, with its handsome, marble-topped mahogany bar and heart-of-pine flooring.

The teal, ivory, and gold backdrop at Troup House Restaurant complements the dining room's white linens, glistening crystal, and rose-patterned carpet. Chef Barnett Blair, who trained at the New England Culinary Institute, presides over a kitchen that features regional specialties. He makes it a daily goal to present natural food simply and elegantly using fresh local ingredients. "A meal here should be as if you are coming to my house to dinner," he said. "And when it's time to go, you don't want to leave."

Barnett collects Old South recipe books. He said that he finds it "emotionally satisfying to deal with Southern cooking," because of its direct link to the land and the seasons.

A not-to-be-missed appetizer is the Grilled Quail Hot N' Brown, served over Smoky Bacon Grits Cakes. It's so delicious that you'll want to schedule a return visit to the St. James to enjoy it again. And for sheer flavor, don't miss the Smokehouse Pork Chop, thick, juicy, wood smoked, and served with Apple and Sour Cherry Chutney. Other popular entrees include Shrimp Parmesan and Sautéed Veal Medallion.

"A dessert should melt away in your mouth," said Barnett. "At least in my mind, that's what it should do." And when you try his Sweet Potato Pecan Praline Bread Pudding, you'll find it does exactly that.

Troup House Restaurant's Sweet Potato Pecan Praline Bread Pudding

1 cup sweet potato, boiled and diced
1 cup sugar
6 eggs, beaten
2 cups plus 2 tablespoons milk
1 tablespoon flour, sifted
pinch of salt

¼ teaspoon ground nutmeg
½ cup light brown sugar
½ cup butter, melted
1 cup pecans, broken
1 tablespoon cinnamon
12 cups day-old French bread, diced
Hard Sauce (recipe below)

Combine sweet potato, sugar, eggs, 2 tablespoons milk, flour, salt, and nutmeg. Add brown sugar, butter, pecans, 2 cups milk, and cinnamon and mix well. Fold in bread and pour into a 9- by 13-inch glass baking dish. Cover with aluminum foil and bake at 250 degrees for 1 hour. Serve warm with Hard Sauce. Serves 15.

Hard Sauce

¼ cup Myers's spiced rum
½ cup unsalted butter, melted

2 cups powdered sugar

Combine all ingredients. Yields about 1 cup.

4-ounce veal tenderloin
seasoned flour
2 teaspoons all-purpose flour
½ cup Pinot Blanc
3 oysters with liquid

2 prepared artichoke hearts,
  quartered
salt and pepper to taste
¾ cup angel hair pasta,
  cooked

Dredge veal in seasoned flour. Place in lightly oiled sauté pan and cook until lightly browned on both sides. Add 2 teaspoons flour, Pinot Blanc, oysters, and artichokes. Reduce and season with salt and pepper. Serve veal and sauce over pasta. Serves 1.

Gaines Ridge

Alabama 10
CAMDEN

$\mathcal{A}$pproaching GainesRidge, a dinner club located two miles east of Camden, I turned into a long driveway lined with moss-draped oak trees to find a two-story, white-columned house with rocking chairs on the front porch. Cedars dotted the surrounding landscape, and red-berried nandinas grew beside the brick steps.

5:30 P.M. until 9:00 P.M.
Wednesday through Saturday

For reservations
(recommended on weekends),
call (334) 682-9707.

One of the area's oldest structures, the home dates to the late 1820s. The Reverend Ebeneezer Hearn, a Methodist circuit rider, owned it at one time, and his family bestowed the home's historical name, The Hearn Place. A veteran of the War of 1812, Hearn is buried in nearby Camden Cemetery.

In 1898, The Hearn Place passed into the family of its current owner, Betty Gaines Kennedy. The Gaines family played a prominent role in Alabama history. Gainesville, Gainestown, the stately antebellum mansion Gaineswood in Demopolis, and Fort Gaines in Mobile Bay all owe their names to this family.

In 1985, when Mrs. Kennedy and her sister Haden G. Marsh founded GainesRidge in the home where they grew up, they chose to use their maiden name for the business. Today, Mrs. Kennedy offers a catering service and operates the dinner club, which seats about a hundred guests in five dining rooms. Family collections of antique china creamers, sugar bowls, gravy boats, and pewter items are displayed on shelves and mantels throughout the Federal-style interior.

"Like many old houses, GainesRidge has its quota of ghosts," Betty said. But she maintains they are benign—even the shrieking woman who has been seen floating past the windows. Other unexplained incidents include the sound of a crying baby, the aroma of pipe smoke when nobody in the house is smoking, and the reflection of a tall, bearded man dressed in black.

In addition to its spiritual presences, GainesRidge provides a gracious atmosphere and delicious food. From Shrimp Bisque to Spinach Salad, from steaks to seafood, everything on the menu is well prepared and delicious. Entrees come with a choice of potato or Herbed Rice. Black Bottom Pie ranks as a favorite on the dessert list.

The Snapper Special and Mama Snooks' Rolls both proved hits with recent guests at my home. And I think you'll enjoy them, too.

GainesRidge's Snapper Special

2 8-ounce red snapper fillets
¼ cup margarine, melted
granulated garlic, parsley,
    and Italian seasoning to
    taste
4 slices lemon or lime
3 tablespoons margarine
½ cup bell pepper, chopped

½ cup green onions, chopped
⅔ cup fresh mushrooms,
    sliced
salt and pepper to taste
cup white wine
2 tablespoons white
    Worcestershire sauce
1 cup crab claw meat, cleaned

Remove skin from fillets and brush both sides with melted margarine. Place fillets on a greased baking pan and sprinkle with seasonings. Place 2 slices lemon or lime on each fillet and bake in a 400-degree oven for 10 to 14 minutes. Remove fruit slices and place fillets under broiler for 2 minutes, monitoring constantly.

To prepare topping, heat a sauté pan, add 3 tablespoons of margarine, and sauté bell pepper and green onions for about 2 minutes. Add mushrooms and sauté for 2 minutes more. Season with salt and pepper. Add wine and white Worcestershire sauce. Cook over medium-high heat for 2 to 3 minutes. Add crabmeat and stir.

Place fillets on heated platters and spoon on crabmeat topping. Replace lemon or lime slices on top of crabmeat. Serves 2.

GainesRidge's Mama Snooks' Rolls

5 cups flour
2 teaspoons baking powder
3 teaspoons salt
1 teaspoon baking soda
2 cups milk

½ cup oil
½ cup sugar
1 package dry yeast
1 cup margarine, melted

Sift 4 cups flour in a large mixing bowl and set aside. Sift together remaining 1 cup flour, baking powder, salt, and baking soda in a separate bowl and set aside. Scald milk, oil, and sugar in a saucepan. Cool to lukewarm. Prepare yeast according to package directions and add to milk mixture, then add milk mixture to 4 cups sifted flour and beat well with a large spoon. Put mixture in a warm place and let rise until double. Add remaining flour mixture and chill for several hours or overnight.

Take all or part of dough and place on a well-floured surface. Knead for 2 or 3 minutes, adding flour if necessary. Roll out to about ¼-inch thickness. Cut with can or cookie cutter to about a 3-inch diameter. Dip half of roll in melted margarine. Fold in half and place on a cookie sheet, buttered side up. Continue until you have desired number of rolls. Let rolls rise for about 30 minutes, then bake at 400 degrees for 15 to 20 minutes until brown. Yields 36 to 40 rolls.

Note: This versatile dough can be dropped by spoonfuls onto a well-greased baking pan, sprinkled with poppy or sesame seeds, and baked as above. It can also be baked in muffin tins or used to make cinnamon rolls.

GainesRidge's Shrimp and Crabmeat Casserole

¼ cup margarine
16 medium shrimp (51-60 count), peeled and deveined
5 or 6 fresh mushrooms, sliced
salt, pepper, and granulated garlic to taste
⅓ cup white wine

¼ cup white Worcestershire sauce
½ cup crab claw meat, cleaned
1 cup Special White Sauce, commercial
½ cup Swiss cheese, grated
¼ cup cheddar cheese, grated
paprika

Melt margarine in a sauté pan over medium-high heat. Add shrimp and sauté for 1 to 2 minutes. Add mushrooms and continue cooking for 2 minutes, stirring constantly. Season to taste with salt, pepper, and garlic. Add wine, white Worcestershire, and crabmeat and cook 2 to 4 minutes until liquid is reduced by half.

Combine Special White Sauce and Swiss cheese in a mixing bowl. Fold in crabmeat mixture, stirring only enough to combine. Pour into individual ramekins or a small casserole. Top with cheddar cheese and sprinkle with paprika. Bake at 375 degrees for 12 to 15 minutes until bubbly. Remove from heat and wait 5 minutes before serving. Serves 3 to 4.

Marengo Plantation

Broad Street
LOWNDESBORO

*A*pproaching Marengo Plantation, I watched lightning dance across the darkening sky—a dramatic backdrop for an evening of fine dining and storytelling in a grand old mansion. Branching pecan trees form an archway over the brick drive, which makes a horseshoe turn at the home's front door.

The restaurant is open only when it is booked for private dinner parties, at which time tables for add-on diners are usually available. For reservations (necessary) and directions, call (334) 278-4442 or (334) 272-8508.

"Welcome to Marengo!" host Art Moody greeted us as we stepped onto the front porch. My husband and I joined fifty other arriving guests to wander through the home's beautifully furnished rooms. After we spent an hour socializing and enjoying drinks and appetizers in the downstairs bar, a bell summoned us to dinner.

Earlier that day, I had dropped in at Marengo and found Chef Mark Moody at work in his inviting country kitchen—the kind that prompts pot-lid lifting to see what smells so good. While stirring a big pot of Cream of Broccoli Soup, to be served that evening, Mark told me about his dinner menu. He then joined me in the library to share some background on this unique restaurant.

Now owned by the Lowndesboro Landmarks Foundation, Marengo has changed hands several times since it was built in 1835 by Dr. John Howard. The house was originally located in Autauga County. Seeking a more prosperous location for his medical practice, Howard dismantled the structure and transported it via rafts across the Alabama River to Lowndesboro, where its numbered boards and bricks were reassembled in 1847.

Located south of Prattville, Lowndesboro was founded by cotton planters in the 1830s and is home to some thirty antebellum structures. The town escaped destruction during the Civil War when Dr. C. C. Reese, the town physician, met Wilson's Raiders to warn them about a local outbreak of smallpox. Although the epidemic was fictional, the ploy worked, and the marauders bypassed Lowndesboro and continued to Montgomery.

Today, Virginia and Art Moody and their sons, Mike and Mark, operate Marengo Plantation as an intimate restaurant for dinner parties and special events. The facility opens when a minimum of thirty guests make a reservation. Once that quota is reached, other diners are accepted on an individual basis, up to a maximum of sixty persons.

Guests dine in the Solarium, the Wicker Room, and the Formal Dining Room. We found place cards and sherry aperitifs waiting at our table and soft music playing in the background. Occasional streaks of lightning illuminated the two-level Solarium.

The Cream of Broccoli Soup tasted as good as it smelled. Next came a refreshing Spinach and Fruit Salad with Poppy Seed Dressing, followed by a palate-cleansing Lemon Sorbet. Our entree, Char-Grilled Tenderloin Fillet, was accompanied by Green Beans, Potato Casserole, and irresistibly light homemade Rolls.

As we savored our Cheesecake, Art stepped onto the dining-room balcony to relate colorful events from Marengo's history. He shared some intriguing ghost stories and invited guests to linger for after-dinner drinks.

After bidding our hosts good night, we departed feeling as if we'd spent an evening at the home of friends. On the front porch, Charlie the Great Dane left his napping spot to extend a friendly paw. The storm had blown over. But even without the lighting's special effects, Marengo still looked stellar.

Marengo Plantation's Spinach and Fruit Salad

10 to 12 ounces fresh spinach, washed
½ cup red cabbage, chopped
15-ounce can mandarin oranges, drained
2 bananas, sliced

8 to 10 ripe strawberries, sliced
3 kiwis, peeled and sliced
2 cups white seedless grapes
1 cup walnuts, chopped
Poppy Seed Dressing (recipe below)

Arrange spinach on salad plates. Top with cabbage, fruits, and nuts. Serve with Poppy Seed Dressing. Serves 8.

Marengo Plantation's Poppy Seed Dressing

⅔ cup apple cider vinegar
1½ cups sugar
½ teaspoon dry mustard
½ teaspoon salt

3 tablespoons onion juice
2 cups cooking oil
3 tablespoons poppy seeds

Start mixer on medium speed and add ingredients in a steady stream in order listed. Cover and refrigerate. Yields about 1 pint.

Debbie Deese

Red's Little School House

Alabama 94 and Gardner Road
GRADY

$\mathcal{T}$he only multiple-choice question you'll need to answer at Red's Little School House comes when it's time to select a dessert from among those listed on the chalkboard.

Housed in the former Hills Chapel Community School built in 1910, the restaurant attracts both locals and travelers to its off-the-beaten-path location south of Montgomery near Dublin and Ramer. A lofty water tower labeled *Pine Level* stands beside the small red school building.

11:00 A.M. until 9:00 P.M.
Wednesday through Saturday

11:00 A.M. until 3:00 P.M.
Sunday

No alcoholic beverages are served. For reservations (needed only for groups), call (334) 584-7955.

After the school bell stopped ringing in 1960, the structure remained vacant except when ladies of the community held quilting bees here. In 1984, Jeanette and Red Deese purchased the old school and toyed with the idea of turning it into an antique shop. Their daughter Debbie persuaded them to start a restaurant instead, maintaining that good, fresh vegetables and barbecue would attract folks to this remote location. More than a baker's dozen years later, the crowds still come, and Debbie makes them glad they did.

Even though the old maps on the walls might bring on a bit of geography-test anxiety and the nation's presidents constitute a solemn gallery atop the chalkboard, this school is one you'll delight in attending. Schoolmarm Debbie, who calls herself "a half-decent guitar player," sometimes sings for the crowd. "Everyone brags on the food," she said, "and laughs at the entertainment."

For the restaurant's bountiful buffet—which features all-you-can-eat home-cooked vegetables—Red grows acres and acres of produce. Debbie and the staff transform the huge harvest into wonderful dishes—Sweet Potato Soufflé, Fried Okra, Squash Casserole, and other delights. The daily menu also features Barbecue, Chicken and Dumplings, and Fried Chicken.

During my visit, I sat at a table where everybody knew everybody else, and they all made me feel right at home. "Did you try the Pickles?" Debbie asked me. "They're delicious and easy to make, too. And you've *got* to taste the Sweet Potato Soufflé."

Debbie has converted two school buses into traveling kitchens, so she can take her catering show on the road for large gatherings. She has cooked for three governors and a president. At catered functions such as political rallies, Red's Fried Cornbread draws long lines, while more exotic appetizers often get bypassed. "It's amazing how many folks ask about Fried Cornbread," noted Debbie. "Since Red's family and staff have eaten it all their lives, they assumed everyone else did, too." Debbie gives instructions for preparing this specialty in the cookbook she compiled for her daughter, Raeanne, to use as a survival manual during her college days. At the urging of customers, Debbie later published it as *Red's Little School House Country Cookbook*.

Sampling even a small portion of the items served here produces a heaped-up plate. Even if you have to skip that dessert question on the chalkboard and pass up the Coconut Cream, Pecan, and Chocolate Pies, you'll give Red's a more-than-satisfactory grade.

Red's Little School House's Easy Rolls

1 cup self-rising flour　　　　*3 tablespoons mayonnaise*
½ cup milk

Combine ingredients and spoon into greased muffin tins. Bake at 425 degrees for about 9 minutes until very light brown; do not overbake. Store unused dough in refrigerator. Yields about 6 rolls.

Red's Little School House's Squash Dressing

2 cups squash, cooked,　　　　*3 eggs, beaten slightly*
　mashed, and drained　　　　*1 can cream of chicken soup*
2 cups cornbread crumbs　　　　*¼ cup margarine, melted*
½ cup onions, chopped　　　　*salt and pepper to taste*

Combine all ingredients and pour into a greased casserole. Bake at 350 degrees for 30 minutes until lightly browned. Serves 8 to 10.

Note: For Corn Dressing, substitute 1 can of whole kernel corn and 1 can of cream-style corn for squash. If desired, you can also substitute 1 can cream of mushroom soup for cream of chicken soup.

1 whole fryer
2- to 3-pound pork roast
chicken broth
2 cups onions, chopped
2 cups potatoes, peeled and
 diced
15-ounce can whole kernel or
 creamed corn

1 can tomato soup
1 cup commercial barbecue
 sauce
2 28-ounce cans diced
 tomatoes in juice
1 cup ketchup
⅓ cup Worcestershire sauce
½ cup prepared mustard

Boil chicken and pork separately until tender. Clean pork carefully and chop; set aside. Cool chicken and save broth. Refrigerate broth and skim fat. Remove and discard chicken skin and bones. Chop chicken and set aside. Place onions and potatoes in a large pot. Cover with chicken broth and boil until done, then add corn, meat, and remaining ingredients. Simmer until heated through. Serves 12 to 14.

Lek's Railroad Thai

Union Station
300 B Water Street
MONTGOMERY

$\mathcal{R}$estored in the early 1980s, Montgomery's Union Station remains a fine example of late-nineteenth-century commercial architecture. The handsome Romanesque Revival building, which occupies a bluff overlooking the Alabama River, ranks as one of the Southeast's largest and most ornate railroad stations.

Montgomery officially came into existence on December 3, 1819, and became the state capital in 1846. Within five years, railroad links had been established with the areas to the northeast and southwest. The town ranked as a major rail junction by the mid-1880s. A decade later, it was served by a dozen railroads, which still used the modest station built in 1860. To boost its public patronage, the Louisville and Nashville Railroad began constructing the handsome Union Station in 1893. The station cost about two hundred thousand dollars. The main building housed waiting rooms on the ground level and offices on the floors above. A train shed, decorated with colored glass in the gables at each end, protected passengers and baggage. By 1894, forty-four passenger trains came through daily. Two flanking buildings completed around 1913 were used for baggage and express items.

Today, Lek's occupies a portion of this historic structure. Here, Anucha Tiemkongkanchna, better known as Lek, offers dishes from his native Thailand. Many of the Asian-inspired menu items are dishes he grew up eating in a household where these foods were prepared routinely. The ingredients for the recipes Lek provided can be found at specialty stores, Asian markets, and the Asian foods section of some supermarkets.

Several trains rolled past my window as I enjoyed Thai Tea, Crystal Noodle Soup, and Spring Rolls with Peanut Sauce. Next came my entree of Pud Thai, with rice noodles topped by shrimp, chicken, and bean sprouts. Other restaurant favorites include Beef Salad (Nurr Num

Lunch
11:00 A.M. until 2:30 P.M.
Monday through Thursday

11:00 A.M. until 2:30 P.M.
Friday.

Dinner
4:00 P.M. until 10:00 P.M.
Friday

11:00 A.M. until 10:00 P.M.
Saturday

For reservations, call (334) 269-0708.

Tok) and Chicken Panang. Most menu items may be ordered mild, medium, hot, or very hot. To add color, Lek garnishes dinner plates with exquisite butterfly and flower creations carved from carrots and radishes.

For an Oriental dining adventure in the original capital of the Confederacy, stop by Union Station, Alabama's largest railway terminal and one of Montgomery's most familiar landmarks.

Lek's Railroad Thai's Spring Rolls

¼ cup ground chicken or pork
2 cups shredded cabbage or
   mixed vegetables (bean
   sprouts, bamboo shoots,
   mushrooms, etc.)
1 rib celery, chopped
½ cup onion, chopped fine

2 tablespoons soy sauce
10 to 12 lumpia wrappers or
   spring roll wrappers
1 egg white
Spring Roll Sauce (recipe
   below)

Combine all ingredients except wrappers, egg white, and Spring Roll Sauce in a mixing bowl and mix well. Place 2 heaping tablespoons of mixture in each wrapper. Fold in sides and roll up as for an egg roll, pressing ends and using egg white to seal. Deep-fry until golden brown. Serve with Spring Roll Sauce. Serves 5 to 6.

Spring Roll Sauce

½ cup sugar
1 tablespoon vinegar

2 tablespoons peanuts,
   ground

Combine sugar and vinegar and boil until sugar melts. Set aside to cool. Add peanuts when ready to serve. Yields ½ cup.

*16-ounce package dried rice
  noodles*
1 tablespoon vegetable oil
1 clove garlic, chopped fine
1 tablespoon beaten egg
*4 to 5 shrimp and/or 4 ounces
  thinly sliced chicken
  breast*

1 tablespoon sugar
2½ tablespoons soy sauce
1 tablespoon vinegar
*2 green onions, cut
  lengthwise into ½-inch
  strips*
*2 tablespoons peanuts,
  ground*
1 cup bean sprouts

Soak rice noodles 1 to 2 hours in warm water. (You will need only ¼ of the noodles for this recipe, but you will not be able to separate the tangle without soaking the entire package.) Heat oil in a pan or wok. Add garlic and stir. When garlic turns light brown, add egg and stir, then add shrimp and/or chicken and stir until meat cooks. Stir in ¼ of the noodles, then add sugar, soy sauce, vinegar, onions, and peanuts and stir until well mixed. Serve with fresh bean sprouts. Serves 1 to 2.

Photo provided by Panache at Rose Hill. Barbara Duke and Shirley Sandy

Panache at Rose Hill

11250 U.S. 80 East
MONTGOMERY

$\mathcal{A}$pproaching Panache at Rose Hill, I turned at the brick columns marking the entrance and followed a winding, tree-lined driveway across the rolling grounds of the 1814 plantation in the Mount Meigs community, located northeast of Montgomery. Originally a four-thousand-acre estate, Rose Hill was built by Henry Lucas, a wealthy landowner

The restaurant is open only when it is booked for private events, at which time tables are usually available for add-on diners. It is open for Easter brunch, on Mother's Day, and on Valentine's Day even if private events are not scheduled. For reservations (necessary), call (334) 215-7620.

in Montgomery County. The estate is listed on the Alabama Historical Register. Its name was inspired by forty surrounding acres of rose gardens.

The present structure, an eleven-room Colonial-style home, sits on a terraced lawn. It was built in 1918 by the Relfe family and later owned and occupied by Mose Smith from 1949 until 1989.

Using their thriving catering business — called Panache — as a springboard to a restaurant partnership, Barbara Duke and Shirley Sandy bought Rose Hill in 1989. They had two goals in mind: preserving the home and offering fine Southern dining and special-occasion facilities in a lovely historical setting.

The two give food demonstrations for culinary shows and various charitable and civic functions. Barbara has demonstrated recipes used at Rose Hill on several local TV shows. Frequent requests for their recipes prompted the team to coauthor a cookbook. So successful was this venture that the first printing sold out in less than six months.

Using cornmeal, peas, squash, buttermilk, and other traditional Southern ingredients, they create a spectrum of delectable dishes like Black-Eyed Pea Pâté, Alabama Caviar, and Catfish Croquettes. The savory Pork Loin Appetizer is a big hit with guests. A recent addition to Panache's repertoire is the Fried Green Tomato and Bacon Burger, which puts a different twist on a couple of old favorites. Typical dinner selections include Prime Rib, Orange Roughy, Beef Tenderloin, Salmon Steak, and Filet Mignon.

My dinner started with a cup of spicy Black-Eyed Pea Soup, topped with scallions and tomatoes and served with a Cornbread Muffin. Then came a salad, followed by Bourbon-Glazed Cornish Hen and vegetables, served with Yeast Rolls. And I couldn't say no to Panache's signature dessert, Buttermilk Pie with Blackberry Sauce.

When it came time to depart, I told Oscar the emu good-bye and stopped to pet a cat on the porch. The pastoral setting makes a perfect home for Panache's resident chickens, geese, goats, and horses.

Panache at Rose Hill's Chocolate Fudge Muffins

2 eggs
1 cup sugar
½ cup butter, melted
½ cup flour, unsifted

⅓ cup cocoa
pinch of salt
2 teaspoons vanilla
½ cup walnuts, chopped

Beat eggs slightly and blend in sugar and butter. Sift together flour, cocoa, and salt and add to egg mixture. Stir in vanilla and nuts. Scoop into greased muffin tins, filling ⅔ full. Bake 20 to 25 minutes at 350 degrees. Let cool completely before removing from tins. Yields 8 muffins.

Panache at Rose Hill's Pork Loin Appetizer

½ cup Dale's Sauce (or any soy sauce–based marinade)
1 tablespoon olive oil
1 teaspoon freshly ground black pepper
3- to 4-pound center-cut boneless pork loin
1 small baguette, preferably sourdough
2 cups butter, softened

2 teaspoons garlic, minced
2 teaspoons fresh basil, chopped
1 teaspoon fresh chives, chopped
1 teaspoon fresh oregano, chopped
1 teaspoon Jane's Krazy Mixed-Up Salt
Horseradish Sauce (recipe follows)

Combine Dale's Sauce, olive oil, and pepper and rub on pork loin. Let stand at room temperature 1 hour. Sear on grill, then bake uncovered in a 350-degree oven for 45 minutes to 1 hour until loin tests done on meat thermometer. Cool at least 15 minutes. Slice baguette into ½-inch slices. Cream together butter, garlic, basil, chives, oregano, and salt. Spread butter mixture on bread and top with slices of pork and Horseradish Sauce. Serves 10 to 12.

Horseradish Sauce

½ pint sour cream
1 tablespoon horseradish
1 teaspoon black pepper

½ teaspoon Krazy Jane's
  Mixed-Up Salt

Combine all ingredients well. Chill in refrigerator for several hours or overnight. Yields 1 cup.

Panache at Rose Hill's Fried Green Tomato and Bacon Burgers

1 giant green tomato
1 cup self-rising white
  cornmeal
1 teaspoon salt
1 teaspoon pepper
vegetable oil
8 slices bacon, cooked crisp
lettuce

1 Vidalia onion, sliced
dill pickle slices
mayonnaise, ketchup, spicy
  mustard, tartar sauce, or
  Horseradish Sauce (recipe
  above) to taste
4 hamburger buns, buttered
  and toasted

Slice tomato into four ½-inch slices. Combine cornmeal, salt, and pepper. Dip tomato slices in water. Shake off excess and firmly pat cornmeal mixture onto each slice. Fry to a golden brown in vegetable oil on medium-high temperature, turning once. Drain tomatoes in a colander lined with paper towels. Assemble burgers by layering tomato slices, bacon, lettuce, onion, pickles, and condiments on buns. Makes 4 burgers.

Sassafras Tea Room

532 Clay Street
MONTGOMERY

On a hill overlooking historic Union Station and the Alabama River stands a striking Victorian home originally known as the Mills House. Constructed around 1888, it now houses Sassafras Tea Room and Antiques.

This was the first home in Montgomery to utilize forced-air heating and a brick-veneer facade. Listed on the National Register of Historic Places, it was built by Alfonzo Mills, a carpetbagger from Michigan. The builder's son, John Proctor Mills, became Alabama's first poet laureate and occupied the home in later years. Located in the historic Cottage Hill district, the venerable structure has twice been threatened by fire. It served as an apartment building several times during recent decades.

Mary and Jim Wallace purchased the historic home in 1990 and spent about a year and a half on its restoration. Hand-carved fretwork in the foyer, hand-painted murals, and period antiques add to the home's ambiance. I found the Tower Room especially intriguing, as do the Wallaces' grandchildren, Katie and Joshua, who enjoy playing up there. In 1995, Sassafras Tea Room expanded to encompass the Next Door House (named by Katie), which dates to around 1900 and was relocated to the Cottage Hill area in the 1920s.

Before, during, or after your meal, you may browse through the antique-filled rooms. Most of the home's pieces are for sale. In the Next Door House, be sure to notice Mary's all-season tree and its interesting decorations.

The Wallaces' daughter, Shannon, and her husband, Russell Houlden, help with the business. Russell shared the restaurant's recipes for Sweet Potato Soufflé, Cornbread Dressing, and Blueberry Crisp.

The menu, which changes daily, features soup and quiche selections plus a variety of specialty sandwiches and salads, such as the popular Crunchy Chicken Salad, served with seasonal fruit. Sassafras also offers such items as Chicken Supreme, Smothered Pork Steak, and Baked Turkey with Russell's Cornbread Dressing. A slice of Chocolate Chip

Lunch
11:00 A.M. until 2:00 P.M.
Sunday through Thursday

11:00 A.M. until 2:30 P.M.
Friday

Dinner
4:00 P.M. until 10:00 P.M.
Friday

For reservations (recommended), call (334) 265-7277.

Pie or Buttermilk Pie puts the proper finishing touch on a Sassafras lunch.

After a good, old-fashioned meal, you may want to walk off some calories and absorb some history at the Alabama State Capitol. This National Historic Landmark housed the original Confederate government in 1861 and has been restored to its Civil War–era appearance.

Sassafras Tea Room's Sweet Potato Soufflé

2 pounds sweet potatoes
1½ cups sugar
1 teaspoon vanilla
1 teaspoon nutmeg
½ cup self-rising flour

2 eggs
½ cup brown sugar
½ cup all-purpose flour
½ cup butter, melted
½ cup walnuts, chopped

Peel and chop sweet potatoes. Place in a pot with ½ inch of water and sprinkle with sugar, vanilla, and nutmeg. Steam until cooked. Mash the candied yams until they are the consistency of cake batter, then add self-rising flour and eggs. Continue to beat until mixture becomes fluffy. Gently spoon into an 8- by 8-inch baking dish. Combine brown sugar and all-purpose flour. Add butter and walnuts and continue to mix; you should end up with a crumbly topping. Place topping on potato mixture and bake uncovered in a preheated 350-degree oven for 45 minutes. Serves 6 to 8.

Sassafras Tea Room's Cornbread Dressing

4 cups cornbread, crumbled
2 cups chicken stock
½ cup parsley
1 cup celery, chopped coarse
1 cup onion, chopped coarse

2 teaspoons rubbed sage
1 teaspoon poultry seasoning
½ teaspoon pepper
¼ teaspoon salt

Combine cornbread and chicken stock. Mixture should be very moist, almost soupy; add more stock if necessary. Add parsley, celery, and onion and mix well. Add seasonings, adjusting to taste. Place mixture in a baking dish and bake in a preheated 350-degree oven for 30 minutes or until done. Yields 4 cups.

Sassafras Tea Room's Blueberry Crisp

21-ounce can blueberry pie
filling
¾ cup sugar

¾ cup flour
¼ cup butter, melted

Place blueberries in a 1½-quart baking dish. Combine sugar and flour in a mixing bowl, then add melted butter. Stir well; you should end up with a crumbly topping. Sprinkle over blueberries and bake at 350 degrees for 30 minutes or until top is browned. Serves 8.

Note: If you use fresh blueberries, place them in a bowl, sprinkle with sugar to taste, and refrigerate overnight.

Hotel Talisi Restaurant

14 Sistrunk Avenue
TALLASSEE

*O*n a corner in the small town of Tallassee stands a charming hotel. Modestly billing itself as "a good place to sleep and eat," Hotel Talisi offers home-style cooking and a yesteryear experience that calls to mind the Roaring Twenties. From its red-carpeted lobby with ceiling fans and crystal chandeliers to its wooden "Superman" phone booth, the structure brims with antiques and nostalgia. The old registration desk, three baby grand pianos (including a 1924

11:00 A.M. until 7:50 P.M.
Monday through Saturday

11:00 A.M. until 2:50 P.M.
Sunday

On Mother's Day, Father's Day, and Thanksgiving, serving time begins at 10:30 A.M.

Alcoholic beverages are not served. For reservations (recommended for large groups), call (334) 283-2769.

version), three upright pianos, and a player spinet add to the ambiance. In the spacious upstairs hall, you'll see Western Union writing desks and an array of seating areas—great for conversation or for curling up with a novel. The individually decorated rooms and suites are furnished with antiques from the early 1900s.

Construction started in 1924, and the hotel was opened in 1928 by its builder brothers, Dan and Jacob Marion Woodall. The Woodall Hotel survived the Great Depression and World War II but suffered an economic setback during the late 1950s. In 1962, Dr. and Mrs. T. M. Patterson purchased the property, made improvements, and changed the name to Hotel Talisi, choosing the original spelling for the area's Creek Indian village along the Tallapoosa River. After operating the hotel almost three decades, the Pattersons sold it to Bob Brown and Roger Gaither, who continue to renovate and refurbish the thirty-two-room structure.

The hotel's spacious dining areas now occupy space that formerly housed clothing shops, a variety store, and a beauty salon. During your visit, take a short stroll across the street to see the hotel's under-the-stars dining oasis, a garden setting with white lights, statuary, and olive trees, designed for special events.

The current crew carries on the hotel's famous family-style buffet, which draws guests from a fifty-mile radius. The daily feast includes Fried Chicken, Baked Chicken with Dressing, Crispy Catfish (on

Fridays), Sweet Potato Soufflé, a medley of fresh vegetables, Cornbread, Hush Puppies, and homemade pies—accompanied by piano or organ music during dinner hours and at lunch on Sunday.

For your next dinner party, try Hotel Talisi's Asparagus Casserole, which is delicious and easy to make. You'll get plenty of compliments, plus requests for the recipe.

Hotel Talisi Restaurant's Asparagus Casserole

14-ounce can asparagus
4 hard-boiled eggs, sliced
2-ounce jar diced pimentos

2 cans cream of mushroom
  soup
1 cup Ritz crackers, crushed
2 tablespoons butter

Arrange asparagus in a buttered 11- by 7-inch casserole. Add a layer of sliced eggs, pimentos, soup, and cracker crumbs. Repeat with 2 more layers, saving about ¼ cup cracker crumbs for topping. Melt butter, stir in remaining crumbs, and sprinkle on top. Bake at 350 degrees for 25 minutes or until bubbly around edges. Serves 8 to 10.

Hotel Talisi Restaurant's Yeast Rolls

1½ cups milk
1½ cups sugar
2 teaspoons salt
¼ cup shortening

6 cups flour
1½ cups lukewarm water
2 tablespoons dry yeast
1 egg

Scald milk. Combine sugar, salt, and shortening and add scalded milk. Add enough flour to make thick dough. Combine water and yeast and add to dough mixture. Beat egg and add to dough, then add remaining flour. Place dough in the bowl of a food processor or mixer. Mix until smooth, using a dough hook. Pour into a greased container and let rise to top 3 times, punching down after first 2 times. Cover and refrigerate; dough is easier to work with when cold. Grease muffin tins and roll out 3 balls for each tin, pressing together in center. Let rise. Bake 10 to 12 minutes at 325 degrees. Store unused dough in refrigerator.

Hotel Talisi Restaurant's Coconut Pie

½ cup butter, softened
1 cup sugar
1½ tablespoons flour
4 eggs
¼ cup buttermilk

1½ cups coconut, grated
15½-ounce can crushed
   pineapple, drained
1 pie shell, unbaked

Cream butter and sugar together. Add flour, eggs, and buttermilk and blend well. Add coconut and pineapple. Pour into pie shell and bake in a preheated 300-degree oven for 1 hour or until center feels firm. Cool and serve. Serves 6.

Heather Rickles

Behind the Glass

168 East Magnolia Avenue
AUBURN

*O*liver Goldsmith unknowingly named the town of Auburn when he wrote this line in *Deserted Village* in 1770: "Sweet Auburn, loveliest village of the plain."

Entering town by way of Interstate 85, I followed a trail of orange tiger paws all the way to the university campus. College towns exude a certain charisma, and Auburn is no exception. After a quick stop for lemonade at Toomer's Corner, a century-old drugstore across from Auburn University's historic main gate, I continued up the street to a unique restaurant/boutique/gallery called Behind the Glass.

10:00 A.M. until 9:00 P.M.
Monday through Saturday

Noon until 9:00 P.M.
Sunday

For reservations (recommended for groups of five or more), call (334) 826-1113.

Donna and Rod Popwell, who own the place, met while working as announcers at Auburn's student radio station. In 1987, they opened their establishment in an old storefront on Magnolia Avenue. The structure had once housed Parker's Department Store, a thriving enterprise in the 1950s. After the owners sold the department store in 1968, the building served at various times as home to a pizza parlor, a deli, and a music shop.

Behind the Glass draws a mix of people: local businessmen, artists, quilters, weavers, and the college crowd. The attractive complex offers tasty food against an ever-changing backdrop of original paintings, pottery, prints, and other works by local and regional artists. "We try not to get too esoteric with what we show," said Rod, "and we change exhibits every six to eight weeks."

House specialties include French Onion Soup, Chicken Croissants, Lasagna, and spicy Cuban Black Beans topped with grated cheddar, diced tomatoes, and scallions.

During your visit, take time to browse through the upstairs boutique, which brims with distinctive apparel, home accessories, and gift items. Afterwards, take a stroll through the Auburn University Historic District. The busy intersection at Toomer's Corner gets blanketed with toilet tissue after each Tiger victory. Sometimes, vehicles are unable to pass for an hour or so during a celebration. Generations of Auburn students wax nostalgic about Toomer's Corner. In fact, the nearby Lovelace Athletic Museum and Hall of Honor contains a replica of this campus landmark, so visitors can experience a football victory complete with the crowd's roar and toilet-tissue streamers even when there's no game in town.

Behind the Glass's Cuban Black Beans

1-pound bag dried black
    beans
1 green bell pepper
1 medium onion
4 to 5 cloves garlic
3 tablespoons olive oil
1 teaspoon salt
¼ teaspoon cayenne pepper
1 teaspoon coarsely ground
    black pepper

30 ounces tomato paste
¼ cup sugar
⅓ cup red wine vinegar
12 cups cooked white rice
grated cheddar, chopped
    tomatoes, and chopped
    scallions for garnish
French bread

Wash beans, place them in a large container, and fill with water, using at least 3 times as much water as beans. Soak overnight. Rinse beans, place them in a stainless-steel pot, and add enough water to cover. Bring to a boil, then reduce heat to low, stirring occasionally. Cook about 2 hours until done; beans should be soft enough to mash between your fingers. Drain.

Chop bell pepper, onion, and garlic and sauté in olive oil for 6 to 8 minutes on medium heat. Add salt, cayenne, and black pepper and stir well. Add mixture to beans, stirring thoroughly. Add tomato paste, sugar, and vinegar. If mixture sticks, do not scrape loose; stir often to minimize sticking. Cover and barely simmer a minimum of 30 minutes until blended.

Serve over rice, using about 60 percent beans to 40 percent rice. Garnish with cheddar, tomatoes, and scallions and serve with French bread. Serves 10 to 12.

Behind the Glass's Pasta Salad

16-ounce package rotini
  pasta
1 bunch green onions
1 bunch parsley (about 1 cup
  without stems)
1½ tablespoons fresh dill
¼ cup fresh Parmesan cheese,
  grated

salt and freshly ground black
  pepper to taste
¼ cup olive oil
2 tablespoons Dijon mustard
1 tablespoon lemon juice
⅓ cup raspberry vinegar
1½ teaspoons garlic powder

Cook pasta according to package directions; rinse in cold water and drain well. Chop onions, parsley, and dill and combine with pasta. Add Parmesan and salt and pepper, then toss. Combine olive oil, mustard, lemon juice, vinegar, and garlic powder in a separate bowl. Add to pasta and mix well. Serves 8 to 10.

Behind the Glass's Chicken Tetrazzini

16-ounce package linguine
½ cup butter
1½ cups mushrooms, sliced
cup flour
1½ cups milk
½ tablespoon tarragon
¾ tablespoon salt

½ tablespoon coarsely ground
  black pepper
1 tablespoon Mrs. Dash
2½ cups cooked chicken,
  chopped
2 cups Monterey Jack cheese,
  grated

Cook pasta according to package directions and let cool. Melt butter in a saucepan. Add mushrooms and sauté until tender. Remove mushrooms from pan with a slotted spoon. Slowly add flour to butter and make a roux. Add milk slowly. Gradually bring to nearly boiling, then add spices. Add chicken, mushrooms, and pasta. Mix well, place in a baking dish, and top with cheese. Cover and bake about 45 minutes at 375 degrees. Serves 10 to 12.

Kendall Manor Inn

534 West Broad Street
EUFAULA

" *No* one loves me. I'm going to the garden and eat worms."

So reads a reflection penciled on a wall in Kendall Manor Inn's towering belvedere. With its commanding view of the local landscape and the river, this vantage point lured generations of Kendall family members, whose poems and ditties go back to June 6, 1894. The builder's grandson wrote, "I, Joe Kendall came up here on Sunday, January 15, 1905, to keep from going to church with my mother."

Dinner
6:30 P.M. until 10:00 P.M.
Friday and Saturday

Dinner is served on weeknights to overnight guests only. Dinner guests can enjoy wine tastings on the last Saturday of each month.

For reservations (required), call (334) 687-8847.

James Turner Kendall, a planter and merchant, purchased building materials for this grand Italianate house before the Civil War but did not complete construction until after the conflict. In addition to the belvedere, distinctive features of the mansion include fifty-two exterior columns, sixteen-foot ceilings, and original gold-leaf cornices in the front and back parlors.

Now a bed-and-breakfast and restaurant owned by Barbara and Tim Lubsen, the home offers large bedrooms with sitting areas and private baths. The rooms are named for places associated with the Kendall family's history: Alabama, England, Georgia, North Carolina, South Carolina, and Virginia.

Serendipity played a role in the Lubsens' discovery of Kendall Manor. After a house-hunting expedition to a nearby town, they decided to swing by Eufaula on the Chattahoochee Trace, a river corridor along the Alabama-Georgia border. When Barbara spotted the house atop a hill and a For Sale sign, she vaulted from the car almost before Tim braked.

While many people might find running such a grand home an overwhelming task, the Lubsens thrive on such challenges. Kendall Manor is the third historic home they've owned.

Overnight guests receive refreshments on arrival, a full breakfast, and a mansion tour. The inn offers seating for thirty-eight in the Kendall Dining Room and the Manor Dining Room. The menu changes weekly, and the Lubsens sometimes invite guest chefs for weekend presentations. Those who dine here experience classic Southern hospitality — and have absolutely no desire to go to the garden and eat worms.

With more than seven hundred buildings on the National Register, Eufaula boasts the state's second-largest concentration of historic homes. A popular time to visit is during the Eufaula Pilgrimage, which showcases local mansions. This annual event takes place in early April and features home tours, antiques shows, concerts, and other festivities.

Kendall Manor Inn's Breast of Chicken with Artichokes and Mushrooms

2 cups fresh mushrooms, sliced
6 tablespoons butter
6 cups water
2 cups white wine
2 carrots, scraped and sliced
2 ribs celery, sliced
1 medium onion, quartered
1 teaspoon salt
1/8 teaspoon pepper
3 large chicken breasts, split, skinned, and boned

14-ounce can artichoke hearts, drained and quartered
4 tablespoons flour
1 cup light cream
1/8 teaspoon white pepper
1 teaspoon dried rosemary
1 teaspoon dried parsley
pinch of nutmeg
2 cups Swiss cheese, grated
paprika

Sauté mushrooms in 2 tablespoons butter and set aside. Combine water, wine, carrots, celery, onion, salt, and pepper in a large stockpot and bring to a boil. Add chicken and bring back to a boil. Simmer 20 minutes, then remove from heat and take chicken out to cool. Reserve stock. Place chicken in a lightly greased 13- by 9-inch pan. Place artichoke hearts and mushrooms on top of chicken. Melt remaining 4 tablespoons butter and whisk in flour to make a roux. Slowly add 1 cup of reserved stock and cream. Stir constantly and bring to a boil. Add white pepper, rosemary, parsley, and nutmeg. Pour sauce over chicken and sprinkle with cheese. Cover and bake at 350 degrees for 20 to 25 minutes. Before serving, garnish with paprika. Serves 6.

Kendall Manor Inn's Romaine Salad

3 small or 2 large heads
   romaine lettuce, washed
   and torn into bite-size
   pieces
1 cup mushrooms, sliced
½ pound bacon, cooked and
   crumbled
¾ cup salad oil
½ cup red wine vinegar

5 tablespoons sugar
2 teaspoons garlic powder
1 tablespoon salt
¼ pound feta cheese with
   sun-dried tomato and
   basil, crumbled
2 cups croutons
¼ cup sesame seeds, toasted

Combine lettuce, mushrooms, and bacon in a large bowl or on individual plates. Combine oil, vinegar, sugar, garlic powder, and salt in a separate bowl and drizzle over salad. Top with cheese, croutons, and sesame seeds. Serves 6 to 8.

Kendall Manor Inn's Heavenly Pumpkin Bread

3 cups sugar
4 eggs, beaten
1 cup oil
⅔ cup water
2 cups pumpkin

1½ teaspoons salt
2 teaspoons baking soda
1 teaspoon cinnamon
1 teaspoon nutmeg
3½ cups flour

Beat sugar, eggs, and oil together. Add water and pumpkin. Combine dry ingredients and add to pumpkin mixture. Stir or beat until blended. Pour into two 9- by 5-inch greased bread pans and bake at 350 degrees for 1 hour or until knife inserted in center comes out dry. Cool 5 minutes on wire rack before removing from pans. Yields 2 loaves.

Garland House

200 North Bell Street
DOTHAN

$\mathcal{P}$eanut Paradise Pie, a Garland House specialty, pays tribute to the region's principal product. Known as the "Peanut Capital of the World," the Dothan area produces 40 percent of the nation's peanut crop. For two fun-filled weeks each fall, the town stages the National Peanut Festival to celebrate the harvest. The packed calendar features a parade, arts, crafts, square-dance sessions by the Goober Gamboleers, and a contest for peanut recipes.

11:00 A.M. until 2:00 P.M.
Monday through Friday

Alcoholic beverages are not served. For reservations (recommended for parties of six or more), call (334) 793-2043.

The latter inspired the creation of Garland House's celebrated dessert, which won first place in a past contest. Although the recipe for Peanut Paradise Pie remains a family secret, visitors will enjoy dipping into the crunchy crust filled with Vanilla Ice Cream and topped with Peanut Sauce and Mocha Sauce. Another popular dessert is the Peppermint Puff, which features a meringue shell with Peppermint Ice Cream and Mocha Sauce.

Other house specialties include Chicken Divan, Chicken Salad, and Crepes. Spiced Tea, served either hot or cold, is a favorite here. Kathy Garrett, who manages the restaurant, says that Nantze Springs Bottled Water, another beverage on the menu, comes from a natural spring on property the Garrett family has owned since the 1920s. "A meal at Garland House is like having lunch at Mom's or Grandmother's," she added.

Attorney A. K. Merrill built the modest bungalow during the early 1900s. The Merrills and their four sons lived here until 1932. The structure later served as a boardinghouse before falling into disrepair. Transforming the neglected home into a restaurant required months of strenuous labor — scrubbing floors, painting walls, hanging wallpaper, ripping up carpet to expose the original wooden floors, and refinishing furniture.

The menu remains much the same as when the restaurant opened in 1976. Jo Garrett and Mary Alice Cleveland started the business and named it by combining parts of their last names. A few years later, Mrs. Garrett bought her partner's interest.

Today, Garland House offers a screened porch (used for dining when weather permits) and five dining rooms. The cash register came from an old general store. Kathy notes that a dollar is the most expensive sum it rings up. Several tables on the premises utilize pedestals made from antique sewing-machine bases.

When providing her recipe for Heavenly Carrots, Kathy said, "This one dish has converted more confirmed carrot haters that any other we know."

Garland House's Strawberry Congealed Salad

12-ounce package sliced
   frozen strawberries,
   undrained
8-ounce can crushed
   pineapple with juice

2 6-ounce packages
   strawberry gelatin
2 cups boiling water
1 cup cold water
1 cup sour cream

Combine strawberries and pineapple in a medium-size bowl; set aside. Dissolve gelatin in boiling water, then add cold water. Pour gelatin into strawberry mixture and combine gently. Pour half of mixture into individual molds, filling each mold halfway. Blend sour cream with remaining strawberry mixture. Once molds have set, fill them with sour cream and strawberry mixture and refrigerate until set. Yields 7 cups.

Garland House's Heavenly Carrots

2 pounds carrots, scraped and
   sliced or cut on the
   diagonal
1 bell pepper, sliced
1 medium onion, sliced
1 can tomato soup
½ cup salad oil

¾ cup sugar
¾ cup vinegar
1 teaspoon prepared mustard
1 teaspoon Worcestershire
   sauce
salt to taste

Boil carrots in salted water until tender, then drain. Layer carrots, pepper, and onion in bowl. Blend remaining ingredients in a separate bowl and pour over vegetables. Refrigerate overnight. Serves 14 to 16.

Poplar Head Mule Co.
Brewpub & Grill

155 South St. Andrews Street
DOTHAN

*F*irst known as Poplar Head, Dothan took its present name in 1885. It was around that time that concerned citizens decided to tone down the town's rowdy image. They hired a marshal and deputies to enforce new laws designed to terminate the saloons' regular Saturday-night brawls.

Several downtown buildings feature murals that depict significant events in the town's history. One such mural covers the entire side wall of Poplar Head Mule Co. Brewpub & Grill. To dip into Dothan's early days, you have only to step inside this establishment, which is also decorated with vintage photos, newspaper excerpts, and other memorabilia. The furnishings include antique tables, chairs, and sideboards and a wooden bar backed by a massive shelf unit from an old-time drugstore. High-backed wooden booths line the brick walls, and antique ceiling fans make slow circles overhead. An enormous moose head mounted over the brewing area peers at patrons.

In the 1890s, Poplar Head Mule Co. played an important role in the town's agrarian economy. Instead of the latest styles in buggies, wagons, and harnesses, the place now provides tasty meals and beer brewed on the premises. Poplar Head's beers include Pale Moon Light, which is crisp and light; Mule Team Gold, a medium-bodied German-type ale; and Downtown Brown, the brewmaster's favorite.

Chef Robert Cazalet—who does double duty as the chef on a local television show—hails from Australia, where he acquired his extensive culinary credentials. "If we missed your favorite dish, let us know," he said, "and if we can, we'll cook it. We do anything here to make people happy."

Cazalet provided his recipe for individual servings of Beef Wellington. For these, he embellishes the crust with the brewpub's initials—and in some cases with the initials of the party who ordered the dish. On the day of my visit, the evening special was Fresh Gulf Snapper, topped with blue crab meat and Lobster Sauce. The menu includes burgers,

11:00 A.M. until 10:00 P.M.
Monday through Wednesday

11:00 A.M. until 11:00 P.M.
Thursday through Saturday

For reservations (recommended on Friday and Saturday evenings and for parties of eight or more), call (334) 794-7991.

ribs, and other casual favorites, along with more elaborate seafood, beef, poultry, and pasta dishes.

Cazalet calls Poplar Head "a brewpub with a touch of class that offers more than sports-bar fare." Those who dine here feel the contentment that a good meal brings, plus a new appreciation for the animal that made a major contribution to the region's early development.

Poplar Head Mule Co. Brewpub & Grill's Ricotta Phyllo Rolls with Walnuts

1½ cups ricotta cheese
½ cup walnut halves
¼ pound Emmenthaler cheese
zest of 2 lemons
⅛ teaspoon ground nutmeg
¼ teaspoon ground cinnamon

¼ cup chives, minced
salt and freshly ground
* pepper to taste*
12 sheets phyllo pastry
2 tablespoons peanut oil or
* vegetable oil*

Mash ricotta with a fork in a large bowl. In a food processor fitted with a shredding disk, grate the walnuts, then the Emmenthaler into the ricotta. Add lemon zest, nutmeg, cinnamon, chives, and salt and pepper and mix well. Cut phyllo sheets in half crosswise and cover with a damp towel to prevent drying out. Working with half a sheet at a time, spread about 2 tablespoons of cheese mixture in a rectangle about 3 inches long by ¾ inch wide, leaving the bottom edge and the sides uncovered. Fold bottom edge over mixture, then fold in sides and roll into a cylinder about 1½ inches in diameter. Repeat with remaining sheets and cheese mixture.

Brush 1 or 2 baking sheets with some of the oil. Arrange rolls on baking sheets about ½ inch apart. Lightly brush pastries with remaining oil. Bake in a preheated 425-degree oven 18 to 20 minutes until golden. Serve either hot or warm while still crisp. Yields 24 rolls.

Poplar Head Mule Co. Brewpub & Grill's
Beef Wellington

1 sheet frozen puff pastry
¼ teaspoon salt
¼ teaspoon pepper
¼ teaspoon dried marjoram,
   crushed
2 4- to 6-ounce beef
   tenderloin steaks

2 tablespoons deli or canned
   mushroom pâté
1 egg white, beaten
Bordelaise sauce
   (commercial or favorite
   recipe)

Thaw pastry according to package directions and set aside. Combine salt, pepper, and marjoram in a small bowl. Rub salt mixture over steaks, coating all sides. Cut pastry in half. Spread 1 tablespoon pâté over 1 side of each steak. Place a steak pâté side down on center of each portion of pastry. Wrap pastry around meat, trim excess pastry from ends, and seal. Place seam side down in a greased, shallow baking pan and brush with egg white. Bake uncovered in a 425-degree oven for about 15 minutes until pastry is golden and meat is desired temperature (about 140 degrees for medium-rare, as determined by a meat thermometer). Serve with Bordelaise sauce. Serves 2.

Poplar Head Mule Co. Brewpub & Grill's
Chocolate Fondue

2 cups dark corn syrup
1½ cups heavy cream
1 pound plus 11 ounces
   semisweet chocolate,
   chopped

assorted sliced fruits such as
   apples, peaches, pears,
   pineapple, strawberries,
   and nectarines

Bring corn syrup and cream to a gentle boil in a saucepan over medium heat. Remove from heat, add chocolate, and stir until completely melted. Arrange assorted fruit on a platter. Use toothpicks or skewers to spear fruit for dipping into warm chocolate. Yields 4½ cups.

The Gift Horse

209 West Laurel Avenue
FOLEY

*M*aking a routine bank trans-action one ordinary day, Jackie McLeod happened to look across the street. There, disguised as a big, old neglected building for sale, stood the high-ceilinged restaurant of her dreams.

She bought the structure, confident that its cracks could be mended and that it would respond to good care — and that she could close up the holes where the sky peeped through.

Throughout the building's surgery and subsequent recovery, Jackie kept reminding herself of the old adage about not looking a gift horse in the mouth. And finally, after all the layers of paint had been sandblasted off the pine walls and ceilings and multiple coats of polyurethane had been applied, The Gift Horse emerged, hale and hearty.

The structure dates to 1912 and opened as the Foley Progressive Club. The membership consisted of the group of men who founded Foley. Mr. Foley—the man for whom the town was named—came from Chicago and wanted a place to hold concerts, dances, and cultural events. When the club opened, four hundred people attended the first dance. "The club's downfall came in the 1930s," Jackie joked, "when they let women join."

The American Legion bought the building in 1937. During World War II, it served as a USO club. In the 1950s, it housed a skating rink. Several hardware stores have also occupied the premises from time to time.

After Jackie and her husband, Dr. Kenneth McLeod, purchased the historic building in 1984 and then restored it, The Gift Horse stopped pacing and broke into full gallop. Jackie's extensive nutrition and catering background—which includes experience as a dietitian at Marshall Field's in Chicago—continues to serve her well at the restaurant she'd wanted for years.

Beyond the restaurant's leaded-glass doors, you'll see the main dining room, which is decorated with large brass chandeliers, lovely stained

Lunch
11:00 A.M. until 4:30 P.M.
Daily

Dinner
4:30 P.M. until 8:00 P.M.
Daily

Alcoholic beverages are not served. For reservations (recommended for groups of ten or more), call (334) 943-3663 or (800) FOLEY, AL.

glass, and green carpet. And you'd better be hungry, because a feast awaits you on the grand mahogany banquet table, which dates from around 1840. Specialties here include Fried Biscuits, Apple Cheese, and Mystery Crab and Shrimp Salad. The buffet of salads, vegetables, meats, breads, and desserts varies daily, but all items are made from Jackie's recipes. Her cookbook, *The Best of The Gift Horse Restaurant*, is available in the gift shop and makes a fitting souvenir.

Before leaving, you may want to visit The Gift Horse Antique Centre, located adjacent to the restaurant.

The Gift Horse's Tomato Pie

1 pie shell, unbaked
3 or 4 medium tomatoes, sliced
1 medium onion, sliced
3 tablespoons flour

pinch of basil or Italian seasoning
½ cup mayonnaise
½ cup Parmesan cheese, grated
1 cup cheddar cheese, grated

Preheat oven to 450 degrees. Prick pie shell with a fork and bake 6 minutes. Remove pie shell and lower oven temperature to 350 degrees. Place a layer of sliced tomatoes and onions in pie shell. Sprinkle with flour and basil or Italian seasoning. Repeat layers 2 or 3 times. Combine mayonnaise and cheeses in a separate bowl and spread on top of pie. Bake about 30 minutes at 350 degrees. Yields 1 pie.

3 cups flour, sifted
4 teaspoons baking powder
¼ teaspoon baking soda
¾ cup sugar
1½ teaspoons salt
1½ cups blueberries
1 cup nuts

2 eggs, beaten slightly
¾ cup milk
½ cup butter, melted
1 tablespoon orange peel,
  grated
½ cup plus 1 tablespoon
  orange juice

Sift together flour, baking powder, baking soda, sugar, and salt. Stir in blueberries, tossing lightly until coated. Beat together remaining ingredients. Add blueberry mixture and stir just until dry ingredients are moistened. Fill greased muffin tins ⅔ full. Bake 20 minutes at 425 degrees. If desired, remove muffins from tins while hot and dip tops in melted butter, then cinnamon sugar. Yields 24 muffins.

Note: For a popular variation, reduce blueberries to 1 cup and add 1 cup chopped pecans.

3 heads red cabbage, shredded
1½ cups bleu cheese,
  crumbled

¾ cup mayonnaise
¼ cup honey mustard

Combine all ingredients just enough to coat. Serves 8 to 10.

The Grand Dining Room

Marriott's Grand Hotel
1 Grand Boulevard
POINT CLEAR

With a rich history dating back to 1847, The Grand Hotel stands serenely at Point Clear (designated *Punta Clara* on the sixteenth-century maps of Spanish explorers). In 1981, the Marriott Corporation purchased this legendary property on Mobile Bay, where the facilities spread over 550 sun-dappled acres.

For a century and a half, this locale has attracted generations of Southern families. The property has survived the Civil War, fire, and hurricanes. One of the resort's buildings, hit by a shell after the Battle of Mobile Bay, served as a hospital for Confederate soldiers. In 1869, a raging kitchen fire caused extensive damage. The first hotel to be called The Grand was built on the original structure's foundation in 1875. Today's Grand Hotel, constructed in 1941, stands on the site of the first resort.

Turning into the driveway, my husband and I admired the lush, landscaped grounds. After checking in, we joined other guests in enjoying one of The Grand's traditions—afternoon tea and homemade cookies, served daily in the wood-paneled lobby. This main building features original heart-pine flooring from the 1875 hotel.

Whether it's strolling under moss-festooned live oaks, biking along meandering lanes, riding horseback, or dancing under the stars, the resort offers plenty of recreational options. The subtropical climate allows guests to golf, play tennis, sail, fish, and enjoy a spectrum of other outdoor activities throughout the year.

As one might expect from the "Queen of Southern Resorts," The Grand offers delectable dining, along with splendid views of Mobile Bay. The Grand Dining Room and the Bay View Room feature a popular Sunday brunch. And for those times when you don't want to change out of your sports togs, you can hop aboard a golf cart and enjoy a casual meal at the Lakewood Club Room on the Azalea Golf Course.

Lunch
Noon until 2:00 P.M.
Daily

Dinner
6:30 P.M. until 9:30 P.M.
Daily

Brunch
11:45 A.M. until 2:00 P.M.
Sunday

Jackets and ties are suggested for men at dinner. For reservations (required for dinner and Sunday brunch), call (334) 928-9201 or (800) 544-9933.

The Grand Dining Room, the resort's largest restaurant, offers seating on two levels. The multicourse dinners might feature seafood, pasta, beef, lamb, veal, or chicken dishes. A three-piece ensemble plays nightly (except Sundays) for guests' dancing and listening pleasure. Couples can get all dressed up for cocktails and dinner, then dance the evening — and some calories — away.

The Grand Dining Room's Uncle Bud's Seafood Gumbo

1 cup onions, chopped
1 cup celery, chopped
1 cup green pepper, chopped
2 tablespoons bacon fat
1 bay leaf
1 teaspoon oregano leaves
1 teaspoon thyme leaves
1/8 teaspoon cayenne pepper
1/2 ounce gumbo filé
2 cups water

14 1/2-ounce can diced
   tomatoes in juice
8-ounce can tomato sauce
1/3 cup brown roux
1/2 pound medium shrimp
4 ounces shucked oysters,
   including liquid
1/2 pound claw crabmeat
3/4 cup okra, cut
salt and pepper to taste

Sauté onions, celery, and green pepper in bacon fat until onions are translucent. Add spices. Add water, tomatoes, and tomato sauce. Bring to a boil, add roux, and cook until mixture thickens. Add shrimp, oysters, crabmeat, and okra and simmer until cooked. Add salt and pepper. Serves 10 to 12.

The Grand Dining Room's
Pecan-Encrusted Red Snapper

*2 pounds red snapper, skin
   and bones removed
salt and white pepper to taste
2 eggs*

*2 cups all-purpose flour
2 cups pecans
¾ cup breadcrumbs
2 tablespoons olive oil*

Cut snapper into 4 equal portions and lightly sprinkle with salt and white pepper. Set aside in refrigerator. Whip eggs and hold in a shallow baking dish. Put flour into a second baking dish. Toast pecans over low heat in a sauté pan until lightly browned. Finely chop pecans in a food processor and blend in breadcrumbs. Dredge snapper in flour, shake off excess, and coat with egg. Next, coat snapper with pecan mixture. Heat olive oil in a sauté pan over medium heat. Sauté snapper 3 to 4 minutes until golden brown, then turn over and repeat. Serves 4.

The Grand Dining Room's Crab Cakes

*4 ounces crabmeat, cleaned
½ cup breadcrumbs
2 tablespoons parsley,
   chopped
2 tablespoons green onions,
   chopped*

*1 egg
1 tablespoon Dijon mustard
2 tablespoons mayonnaise
pinch of salt
pinch of white pepper
flour*

Combine crabmeat, breadcrumbs, parsley, and green onions in a mixing bowl. Add egg, mustard, mayonnaise, salt, and white pepper. Divide mixture into 4 equal portions and pat into cakes. Refrigerate for 1 hour. Lightly dust cakes with flour and sauté over medium-high heat for 2½ minutes per side until golden brown. Yields 4 cakes.

The Wash House Restaurant

U.S. 98 one mile south of Marriott's Grand Hotel
POINT CLEAR

$\mathcal{H}$alf the fun in finding The Wash House Restaurant lies in discovering the adjacent Miss Colleen's House, a special treat for candy lovers. Edward Brodbeck spent three years on the home's construction, choosing a classical style with high, open ceilings and galleries designed to catch the prevailing breezes. He se-

Dinner
5:00 P.M. until 9:00 P.M.
Sunday through Thursday

5:00 P.M. until 10:00 P.M.
Friday and Saturday

For reservations (recommended), call (334) 928-1500.

lected the timber from near Moss Point, Mississippi, and floated the logs through the Mississippi Sound and across Mobile Bay to be hand-sawed into lumber on the site.

Inside the 1897 gingerbread house is the Punta Clara Kitchen, where you can observe the candy-making process and sample homemade confections developed by the Brodbeck family. The gift shop on the premises features Fudge, Pecan Butter Crunch, Divinity, English Toffee, Chocolate-Covered Bourbon Balls, Buckeyes (balls of creamy peanut butter hand-dipped in chocolate), and more. After sampling the goods, you can wander along the hallway of this captivating Victorian home and peer into rooms still furnished as they were at the turn of the century.

Behind the historic home stands a weathered structure of cedar and cypress that originally served as a kitchen, laundry, and wine cellar for the main dwelling. Surrounded by live oak trees dripping with Spanish moss, it now houses The Wash House.

While dining in this white-tablecloth restaurant, you might bump into a governor, an ambassador, or a celebrity. Dolly Parton, Stacy Keach, Jimmy Buffet, and Steven Seagal have all visited The Wash House, says Wanda Taylor, who owns this family-operated eatery with her husband, John. Their daughter, Joni Baecher, serves as chef, and Joni's daughter, Casey, is the chef's assistant. "Joni has always loved to cook," said Wanda, "and she has a divine talent for it."

The appetizers range from Crab Claws, Fried Crawfish Tails, and Artichoke Hearts to Escargots. Noted for its seafood, steaks, continental specialties, and sophisticated sauces, the restaurant also features Soft-Shell Crabs grown exclusively for The Wash House and served in season. Shrimp and oyster selections and the Seafood Platter—which includes fish, shrimp, oysters, and crab claws—are perennial favorites here.

Joni prepares Old South dessert selections daily. She generously shared her recipe for delicious Bread Pudding with Southern Comfort Nutmeg Sauce.

The Wash House Restaurant's French Onion Soup with Sherry and Mushrooms

6 pounds white onions, peeled and sliced thin
½ cup butter
½ cup olive oil
8 cups beef stock
1 tablespoon white pepper
2 tablespoons garlic, chopped

2 tablespoons Italian seasoning
1 cup cream sherry
1½ pounds fresh mushrooms, sliced
croutons
Parmesan cheese

In a large soup pot, sauté onions in butter and olive oil until they begin to caramelize. Add beef stock and bring to a simmer. Season with white pepper, garlic, and Italian seasoning. Simmer on low heat for 45 minutes. Add sherry and mushrooms and simmer another 15 to 20 minutes until mushrooms are tender. Serve hot with croutons and Parmesan cheese. Serves 12.

½ cup butter, softened
16-ounce loaf French bread, sliced thin
1 cup raisins
12 eggs
2¼ cups sugar
2 teaspoons vanilla
5½ cups milk, scalded
Southern Comfort Nutmeg Sauce (recipe below)

Lightly butter 1 side of bread slices. Place a single layer of slices buttered side down in a 9- by 13-inch glass baking dish. Sprinkle with raisins. Repeat with another layer of bread slices, buttered side down. Beat eggs with sugar and vanilla. Gradually add milk and mix well with a wire whisk. Strain to remove any eggshells or unblended egg. Pour milk over bread layers and let stand 30 minutes at room temperature. Bake 50 to 60 minutes in a water bath in a preheated 350-degree oven until a knife inserted into the center comes out clean. Serve warm with Southern Comfort Nutmeg Sauce. Serves 12.

Southern Comfort Nutmeg Sauce

1 cup dark brown sugar
2 tablespoons extrafine flour
1¼ cups hot water
½ cup butter, cut into ¼-inch pieces
1 teaspoon nutmeg
1 tablespoon vanilla
¼ cup Southern Comfort

Thoroughly blend sugar and flour in a small saucepan. Gradually add water a small portion at a time. Cook over low heat until sauce begins to thicken. Add butter 1 piece at a time until all butter melts. Bring to a gentle boil. Remove from heat and stir in nutmeg, vanilla, and Southern Comfort. Yields 2 cups.

Bienville Bistro

358 Dauphin Street
MOBILE

*G*hosts, you say? Bienville Bistro's brochure acknowledges this possibility with descriptions of past "spiritual guests."

When John McGuire constructed the three-story Federal-style building in 1852, he unknowingly built on the site of an Indian and Spanish burial ground. The McGuire family lived in apartments above its first-floor store until 1885. Then the store was converted to a shirt factory and dressmaking shop, then to a millinery. Mohana Kalifeh purchased the building in 1926 and operated a store here until 1960, after which the venerable structure fell into disrepair until John Word transformed it into a fine-dining establishment in 1977. Soon afterward came reports of mysterious sightings and occurrences, but these did not deter patrons. The restaurant remained popular until Word closed it in 1993.

6:00 P.M. until 9:00 P.M.
Tuesday through Thursday

6:00 P.M. until 10:00 P.M.
Friday and Saturday

For reservations (recommended, especially on weekends), call (334) 694-0040.

Then along came current owner Chakli Diggs, who in 1992 had opened downtown Mobile's first *nouvelle cuisine* restaurant. In 1996, he relocated the bistro to the historic McGuire-Word Building, which offered expanded kitchen facilities and dining rooms. Guests can now enjoy dinner at Bienville Bistro, lunch in the adjacent courtyard (called Rendezvous), and drinks and music in the Speakeasy, located downstairs. The complex also offers banquet facilities on the third floor.

Chakli describes his cuisine as having "a continental base with local influences," and he vows to keep the menu "fresh, varied, and interesting." A typical evening's offerings include five appetizers, three salads, five entrees, and exquisite desserts like Hazelnut and Chocolate Terrine, prepared by a gifted pastry chef.

I chose the Angel Hair Pasta with Mussels, Scallops, and Whitefish. My husband shared a taste of his Grilled Grouper—also delicious. We sampled two sinfully spectacular desserts—Crème Brûlée (with a blueberry surprise waiting at the bottom) and Spring Cake.

After dinner, we descended a flight of stairs and followed a long, dimly illuminated brick hallway to the Speakeasy, where Chakli joined us. Born in Ethiopia and schooled in Germany, he speaks five languages. A "genetic obligation" brought him to the Port City, where his mother and sister live. Chakli says he had always wanted a restaurant of his own — with or without ghosts.

We didn't see any ghosts during our evening at Bienville Bistro, but then we didn't visit the third floor, an area reserved for special occasions — and maybe special guests.

Bienville Bistro's Grilled Tuna with Spinach, Tomatoes, and Capers

½ cup butter
4 cups fresh spinach
1 cup green beans, blanched
¼ cup fresh cilantro, chopped
2 tablespoons fresh lime juice
1 tablespoon capers, drained
4 8-ounce tuna steaks

olive oil
1 tablespoon fresh thyme, chopped
1½ teaspoons black pepper, ground coarse
salt to taste

Brown butter in a skillet over medium heat. Add spinach, green beans, cilantro, lime juice, and capers and toss until just heated through. Keep warm. Brush tuna steaks with oil and sprinkle with thyme, pepper, and salt. Grill about 3 minutes on each side until opaque. Slice steaks into ½-inch strips. Bunch up spinach in center of 4 plates and top with tuna slices. Serves 4.

Bienville Bistro's Jumbo Sea Scallops Cajun-Marsala

1 tablespoon olive oil
1 tablespoon peanut oil
3 jumbo sea scallops
2 cloves garlic, minced
½ teaspoon Seafood Magic or
   other commercial seafood
   seasoning

½ teaspoon flour
¼ cup Marsala
juice of ½ lemon
⅓ cup scallop juice
⅓ cup whipping cream
1 sprig parsley, chopped

Heat olive oil and peanut oil in a sauté pan over medium heat. Add scallops and sauté all sides for about 3 minutes. Add garlic and toss another minute. Add Seafood Magic and toss scallops to coat. Sprinkle flour to coat, then add Marsala and let simmer for 1 minute. Add lemon juice and scallop juice and stir for 1 minute. Add whipping cream and reduce for 2 minutes. Remove from heat and pour into a shallow bowl. Sprinkle with parsley to garnish. Serves 1.

Note: This dish can be broiled and topped with grated mozzarella.

Drayton Place

101 Dauphin Street
MOBILE

he handsome Van Antwerp Building, Alabama's first sky-scraper, stands on the corner of Dauphin and Royal Streets in the heart of downtown Mobile. Reputed to be the first skyscraper in the Southeast, the building was designed by George B. Rogers and is listed on the National Register of Historic Places. Construction started in 1906, and completion came two years later.

11:00 A.M. until 10:00 P.M.
Monday through Thursday

11:00 A.M. until midnight
Friday and Saturday

For reservations (recommended for parties of six or more), call (334) 432-7438.

Garet Van Antwerp and his sons commissioned the towering structure to house their family-operated drugstore, which had occupied this prominent corner since 1884. Still family owned, the building is now home to Drayton Place.

Approaching the restaurant, my husband and I heard the sounds of jazz. A big thermometer marks the front door, and some of the building's original mosaic tiles remain near the entry. We admired the elegant interior, with its two massive central columns and grand architectural features. Hand tooled by Italian artisans, the lofty ivory and gold ceiling with ornamental molding features three chandeliers suspended on brass chains. Running the length of the dining room, the former soda fountain and prescription counter now functions as a bar. An upstairs dining area accessed by marble stairs in the rear makes a fine vantage point for seeing the setting in its entirety.

The Van Antwerp Building stood vacant or only partially utilized for many years until Eric Buckner recognized its potential. Previously affiliated with a historic hotel and the Charlotte City Club in Charlotte, North Carolina, Buckner saw an opportunity to open his own pub.

The interior renovation brought to light features that had been concealed for years. To expose the rich mahogany woodwork behind the bar, Buckner spent countless hours scraping down to the original wood — "therapy scraping," he calls it. Each time he returned from a bank-funding quest with a negative response, he attacked the restoration with more vigor.

Buckner describes his cuisine as "Southern coastal" with Creole and Southwestern influences. "I want to take the starch out of fine dining," he says, "and present meals without the formality or expensive prices."

The weekend entertainment at Drayton Place features Mobile's best jazz artists and guest musicians from around the country. The restaurant offers an all day, same-price menu, with selections changing every six months. Some of the popular items here are Hot Crab Dip, Blackened Snapper with Creamy Shrimp Creole Sauce, and Shrimp and Grits. The latter features baked Southern grits cakes topped with jumbo gulf shrimp, Creole sausage, and a spicy wine sauce. Among the desserts, the light and delicious Tiramisu is the favorite, with Kentucky Bourbon Pie running a close second.

Drayton Place's Grilled Tuna with Spinach Pesto Sauce

6 cups fresh spinach, washed
    and trimmed
¼ cup parsley
½ cup pine nuts

2 cloves garlic
⅓ cup olive oil
½ cup Parmesan cheese
2 8-ounce tuna steaks

Mix spinach, parsley, pine nuts, garlic, olive oil, and Parmesan in a mixer for 1 minute. Chill for 10 minutes. Lightly grill tuna, then cover with chilled pesto. Serves 2.

Drayton Place's Korean Barbecued Shrimp

½ cup Worcestershire sauce
hot sauce to taste
¼ cup lemon juice
2 cloves garlic

10 flakes rosemary
14 shrimp (16-20 count),
    peeled and deveined
rice or pasta

Place Worcestershire, hot sauce, lemon juice, garlic, and rosemary in a sauté pan and bring mixture to a boil. Add shrimp to pan and cook on each side for 30 seconds. Serve over rice or pasta. Serves 2.

Drayton Place's Jack Daniel's Rib-Eye

2 12-ounce rib-eye steaks
¾ cup beef stock
⅓ cup brown sugar

¼ cup Jack Daniel's
2 tablespoons cornstarch

Grill steaks as desired. Bring beef stock, brown sugar, and Jack Daniel's to a boil in a saucepan. Add cornstarch. When sauce thickens, pour over steaks. Serves 2.

Justine's Courtyard
& Carriageway

80 St. Michael
MOBILE

As I sat at a table in the brick-lined carriageway talking to Justine's owners, Matt and Regina Shipp, I tried to visualize the historic setting back in 1852. Originally a passage for horse-and-buggy traffic, the carriageway leads to Justine's courtyard and once served as a stabling facility.

Instead of the clatter of hooves reverberating against the brickwork, today's sounds lean toward live jazz—especially during Sunday's champagne brunch. The carriageway and the courtyard make a pleasant backdrop for sipping mimosas and savoring the ambiance of the Old South.

Lunch
11:30 A.M. until 2:00 P.M.
Wednesday through Friday

Dinner
5:00 P.M. until 9:00 P.M.
Sunday, Monday, and Wednesday

5:00 P.M. until 10:00 P.M.
Thursday through Saturday

Brunch
11:00 A.M. until 3:00 P.M.
Sunday

For reservations,
call (334) 438-4535.

The landmark building that houses Justine's originally served as the Bank of Mobile. In fact, two of the bank's old vaults remain on the premises. The building later served as headquarters for a printing company.

The restaurant's decor is one of quiet elegance. A pair of sofas flank the entry, which leads to a large central section. The adjacent dining areas feature romantic lighting.

Chef Matt Shipp brings both credentials and panache to food preparation and presentation. He comes from a family with more than six decades of experience in the restaurant business. As a youngster, Matt "played around in the kitchen" of his family's restaurant in Fort Walton Beach, Florida, little suspecting he might be practicing for a grown-up career. He went on to become an honors graduate of one of the world's finest cooking schools, the Culinary Institute of America in Hyde Park, New York. Afterwards, he polished his culinary prowess in leading restaurants in New York and New Orleans.

For starters, consider Justine's Crab Cakes, or perhaps the Curried Escargots with Rosemary over French Pastry. The Whiskey Smoked

Shrimp appetizer arrives at diners' tables in Belgian endive leaves. The entree choices include fresh pasta, seasonal seafood, fowl, beef, and lamb. The Grilled Rack of Lamb with Hot Pepper Glace lends a spicy twist to a traditional favorite.

Justine's offers an extensive wine selection. In fact, the menu descriptions suggest wine choices that best complement Matt Shipp's creations.

Justine's Courtyard & Carriageway's Crab Cakes

1 pound lump crabmeat
1 egg
1 teaspoon dry mustard
2 teaspoons Worcestershire
   sauce
1½ teaspoons mayonnaise

½ teaspoon paprika
2 tablespoons butter, melted
¾ cup breadcrumbs
⅛ cup parsley, chopped
¼ cup pimentos, chopped
lemon juice, Tabasco sauce,
   salt, and pepper to taste

Combine all ingredients and shape into 8 cakes. Sauté in vegetable oil. Serves 8 as an appetizer.

Justine's Courtyard & Carriageway's Butter Bean Cakes

16-ounce bag dried butter
   beans
4 leeks, chopped
4 red peppers, chopped
4 cloves garlic, minced
2 teaspoons freshly squeezed
   lemon juice

1 cup feta cheese
¼ teaspoon Tabasco sauce
1 cup breadcrumbs
vegetable oil
2 cups shiitake mushrooms,
   chopped
¼ cup butter

Soak butter beans overnight, then cook according to package directions. Drain beans and allow to cool. Combine beans with half of the leeks, half of the red peppers, half of the garlic, lemon juice, feta cheese, Tabasco, and breadcrumbs in a large bowl. Form into about 10 patties. Cakes should hold together; if they do not, add more breadcrumbs. Sauté cakes in vegetable oil and set aside. Combine remaining leeks, red peppers, and garlic with mushrooms in a saucepan and sauté in butter until translucent. Place on top of bean cakes. Yields about 10 bean cakes.

Justine's Courtyard & Carriageway's
Grilled Rack of Lamb with Hot Pepper Glace

1 New Zealand lamb rack
2 cups vinegar
⅓ cup sugar

⅓ red bell pepper, chopped
⅓ green bell pepper, chopped
½ teaspoon habanero chile, chopped

Season lamb as desired and grill to desired doneness. Set aside. Combine vinegar, sugar, peppers, and chile and bring to a boil. Serve over lamb. Serves 4.

Mayme's

Malaga Inn
359 Church Street
MOBILE

*M*obile, Alabama's oldest city, is always enchanting, but it is especially so in spring, when thousands of azaleas explode into every glorious shade of pink on the color wheel. Local lore traces the flowering shrubs' origin back to the mid-1700s, when Mobile was a French colony. Today, the flamboyant azaleas make the Church Street area, DeTonti Square, Oakleigh Garden, Spring Hill, and other historic districts more gorgeous than ever. And as always, centuries-old live oaks spread their canopies to frame everything—from city streets to mansions and commercial buildings.

Breakfast
7:00 A.M. until 10:00 A.M.
Daily

Lunch
11:00 A.M. until 2:00 P.M.
Monday through Saturday

Dinner
6:00 P.M. until 10:00 P.M.
Monday through Saturday

For reservations (recommended), call (334) 438-4701.

In the heart of downtown Mobile stands the charming Malaga Inn—actually twin mansions flanking a central courtyard. Enveloped by silvery Spanish moss hanging from the branches of live oaks, the mirror-image town houses date to 1862. They once belonged to sisters, whose families shared the connecting patio. In 1967, the historic structures were joined and converted into an inn with individually decorated rooms and suites. The Malaga Inn boasts of having antiques, high ceilings, and spacious dressing areas, and many rooms retain their original hardwood floors.

Mayme's, the courtyard restaurant at the inn, serves exceptional French, European, and New Orleans cuisine. You'll enjoy dining in either the cozy Carriage House, with its appealing floral decor and comfortable upholstered chairs, or under the stars in the Garden Courtyard, with its flowing fountain, umbrella-topped tables, lofty gaslights, and surrounding galleries of ornamental ironwork.

Executive Chef Michael Cunningham's fare is as elegant as the Malaga Inn's heritage. You might try an appetizer of Shrimp Rémoulade or Crepe d'Orleans, filled with andouille sausage, crawfish, spinach, and cream cheese. For your entree, you might select the wonderful Grilled Herb-Crusted Lamb Rack with Cilantro Pesto and Smoked Tomato Salsa. Other choices might include Duckling, Cajun Pork Loin,

Crawfish Etouffée, Potato-Crusted Snapper, or Filet Rubert, a filet mignon served with Garlic Cream Sauce and topped with fresh crabmeat.

Mayme's is a great place for lingering over coffee and dessert. The dessert selections vary with the season, but Eggnog Flan remains a holiday favorite.

Mayme's Grilled Herb-Crusted Lamb Rack with Cilantro Pesto and Smoked Tomato Salsa

1 bunch cilantro
¼ cup pine nuts, toasted
3 cloves garlic, minced
1 teaspoon cumin seed,
    ground and toasted
1 cup olive oil

¼ cup Romano cheese, grated
2 1¼-pound baby lamb racks
Smoked Tomato Salsa
    (recipe follows)
Southeastern-Style Corn
    Pone (recipe follows)

Mince cilantro in a food processor until fine. Add pine nuts, garlic, and cumin. With processor running, slowly drizzle in olive oil until combined. When consistency is smooth, add Romano.

Rub each lamb rack with 1 tablespoon pesto. Wrap in plastic and chill 2 hours. Preheat grill and cook lamb racks about 8 minutes until medium-rare, turning frequently so they do not burn. Serve with Smoked Tomato Salsa and Southeastern-Style Corn Pone. Serves 2.

Southeastern-Style Corn Pone

6 ears fresh corn, cut off the
    cob (or 10-ounce package
    frozen corn)
¾ cup heavy cream

1 small onion, minced
3 large eggs, beaten
salt and pepper to taste
¼ cup softened butter

Combine 1½ cups corn and cream in a blender. Blend until corn is coarsely ground. Pour into large mixing bowl. Add remaining ingredients and mix thoroughly. Pour into a 4- by 8-inch baking dish and bake at 350 degrees for 40 minutes. Serve with Herb-Crusted Lamb Rack and Smoked Tomato Salsa.

Smoked Tomato Salsa

6 medium tomatoes, cut in
   half
1 small serrano chile
1 small red onion, cut in half
2 tablespoons virgin olive oil
3 sprigs parsley, chopped

1 clove garlic, minced
¼ teaspoon chili powder
1 teaspoon Cilantro Pesto
   (recipe above)
juice of 1 lime
salt and pepper to taste

Combine tomatoes, whole serrano chile, and red onion in a large mixing bowl. Combine olive oil, parsley, garlic, chili powder, and Cilantro Pesto in a separate bowl. Pour over vegetables and marinate for 1 hour. Place vegetables cut side down on a preheated grill. Cover and let smoke for 10 minutes on very low heat. Remove to a mixing bowl and let cool. Cut vegetables fine. Add lime juice and salt and pepper. Garnish lamb racks with salsa. Yields 2 cups.

Mayme's Eggnog Flan

1 cup sugar
4 eggs, beaten
14-ounce can sweetened
   condensed milk

1¾ cups eggnog
pinch of salt
¼ teaspoon cloves, ground

Place sugar in a medium-size skillet over medium-high heat. Stir with a wooden spoon about 5 minutes until sugar turns golden brown; do not let it turn dark brown. Pour this caramelized sugar into 8 soufflé cups, tilting and turning to coat sides and bottoms. Let cool. Whisk eggs with remaining ingredients and pour into caramel-lined cups. Place cups in a baking or roasting pan with sides taller than 2 inches. Add boiling water halfway up sides of cups. Bake in a preheated 300-degree oven for 45 to 50 minutes, until a knife inserted near the center comes out clean. Remove pan from oven and remove cups from hot water. Let cool completely before removing from molds. Serves 8.

Spot of Tea

310 Dauphin Street
MOBILE

Several of Mobile's downtown restaurants share similar physical traits, but each has a personality all its own. Take Spot of Tea, located across from Cathedral Square. This attractive eatery occupies a landmark 1836 building that has served at various times as a department store, a dry cleaner, a Sunday school, and offices. "The upstairs apartments were used as multifamily dwellings for shopkeepers, who worked in retail downstairs," said Ruby Moore.

Ruby and her son, Tony, own Spot of Tea, which offers breakfast, brunch, lunch, tea, and special-events catering. Guests enter through a central gift shop flanked by the restaurant's two dining rooms: the Victorian Room and the Carriage Way. The latter features an arched ceiling and original floors and brick walls. A dressing-room mirror from the old department store occupies a special spot, and another wall showcases a handsome mural depicting Dauphin Street, painted by Ruby's daughter with the help of an artist colleague. The restaurant's opposite side — the Victorian Room — is an attractive garden-type room, light and airy with a floral decor.

"Tony always loved to cook," said his mother, "and starting this restaurant was his idea." Inspired by a (reluctant) visit to a teahouse out of state, he immersed himself in research about tea. Tony then found the ideal location and persuaded his mother to join him in the venture.

"Our big priorities are freshness and temperature," Ruby said. "Hot is hot and cold is cold."

Blackened Chicken Caesar Salad and Gourmet Potato Salad (the coppery color comes from paprika) are often requested by patrons. Another favorite is the Fresh Fruit Pizza Pie. On patriotic holidays, Ruby bakes the crust in a rectangle and decorates it like a flag by topping cream cheese with strawberries and blueberries. Other menu selections include Eggs Benedict, omelets, soups, sandwiches, and salads.

7:00 A.M. until 2:00 P.M.
Daily

Brunch
10:00 A.M. until 2:00 P.M.
Sunday

Parties of ten or more can reserve space for English tea or high tea in the afternoons and evenings.

Smoking is not permitted. No alcoholic beverages are served. For reservations (needed only for groups of six or more), call (334) 433-9009.

Of course, many patrons favor the specialty coffees and teas. Tea flavors range from Cranberry, Elderberry, Mango Mist, and Wild Blackberry to Peppermint, Earl Gray, and more. All in all, Spot of Tea is a perfect place for sipping refreshing Peach-Apricot Tea and enjoying life.

Spot of Tea's Gourmet Potato Salad

2½ pounds medium-size red
  potatoes
½ cup sour cream
¾ cup mayonnaise
1 bunch green onions,
  chopped fine

½ cup bacon bits
1 teaspoon garlic powder
2 tablespoons fresh dill,
  minced
salt and pepper to taste
1 teaspoon paprika

Wash potatoes but do not peel. Cut potatoes into bite-size cubes. Boil until tender but do not overcook. Add remaining ingredients and mix well. Yields about 8 cups.

Spot of Tea's Chicken Salad

3 pounds boneless, skinless
  chicken breasts
8-ounce package cream
  cheese, softened
1 cup mayonnaise

4 ribs celery, chopped fine
celery salt, salt, and pepper to
  taste
½ cup pecan pieces

Boil chicken until tender, then cool under cold water and cut into bite-size pieces. Combine cream cheese and mayonnaise, then add celery, spices, and pecans, blending well. Add chicken. If salad is not creamy enough, add more mayonnaise. Serves 10.

20-ounce package
   refrigerated sugar cookie
   dough
1 cup confectioners' sugar
8-ounce package cream
   cheese, softened

1 teaspoon vanilla
fresh strawberries, halved
bananas, sliced and dipped in
   lemon juice
kiwi, peeled and sliced
pineapple, sliced

Spray a pizza pan with Pam. Press cookie dough to fit pan. Bake at 350 degrees for about 15 minutes until golden brown. Cool completely. Use an electric mixer to blend sugar, cream cheese, and vanilla. Spread mixture onto crust and dress pizza with fruit. When ready to serve, slice into wedges. Yields 1 fruit pizza.

Index

Patty's Sunrise, Mountain Inn
Restaurant 20
Petite Butter Cookies with Lemon
Curd, Covington's 32
Rum Raisin Ice Cream, Highlands
Bar & Grill 80
Sweet Potato Pecan Praline Bread
Pudding, Troup House
Restaurant 123
White Chocolate Brownies,
Provence Market 64

Pies:

Banana Split Pie, Shelly's Iron
Gate 44
Coconut Pie, Hotel Talisi
Restaurant 152
Peach Cobbler, Little River
Cafe 16

Entrees

Fowl:

Baked Chicken Pulley Bone,
Sweetbriar Restaurant 12
Breast of Chicken with Artichokes
and Mushrooms, Kendall Manor
Inn 160
Chicken Cordon Bleu, Cragsmere
Manna 24
Chicken and Shrimp Sauté, Tally-
Ho Restaurant 120
Chicken Lafayette, LOUISIANA
The Restaurant 59
Chicken Tetrazzini, Behind the
Glass 156
Stuffed Breast of Chicken, Barrett's
Brewpub & Eatery 99

Meat:

Apricot-Rosemary Pork Tenderloin, Covington's 31

Beef Stroganoff, Mountain Inn
Restaurant 20
Beef Tenderloin Greek-Style, The
Bright Star 96
Beef Wellington, Poplar Head
Mule Co. Brewpub & Grill 168
Garlic-Rubbed Tenderloin with
Roasted Red Pepper Sauce,
Court Street Cafe 52
Grilled Herb-Crusted Lamb Rack
with Cilantro Pesto and Smoked
Tomato Salsa, Mayme's 195
Grilled Rack of Lamb with Hot
Pepper Glace, Justine's Court-
yard & Carriageway 192
Jack Daniel's Ribeye, Drayton
Place 188
Jambalaya, Ca-John's Faunsdale
Bar & Grill 111
Roasted Rack of Lamb with Black
Olive Sauce, Johnston Street
Cafe 39
Sautéed Veal Medallions, Troup
House Restaurant 124
Seared Ribeye with Mushrooms
and Onions, The Olde
Warehouse 7

Seafood:
Baked Atlantic Salmon, The
Victoria 4
Chipotle Grilled Grouper, Cobb
Lane Restaurant 76
Crab Cakes, The Grand Dining
Room 176
Crawfish Etouffée, Highlands Bar
& Grill 79
Crawfish Pie, Ca-John's Faunsdale
Bar & Grill 111
Crazy Cajun, The Landmark 67
Grilled Tuna with Spinach Pesto

Salads

Salsas, Sauces, Dressings, Relishes, and Gravies

Southern Comfort Nutmeg Sauce,
The Wash House
Restaurant 180
Spring Roll Sauce, Lek's Railroad
Thai 139
Wine Butter Sauce, The Victoria 3

Sandwiches
Fried Green Tomato and Bacon
Burgers, Panache at Rose
Hill 144

Soups and Stews
Camp Stew, Red's Little School
House 136
Cabbage and Potato Soup, Moun-
tain Inn Restaurant 19
Corn and Wild Rice Soup, The
Globe 108
Chicken and Rice Soup,
Trowbridge's 55
Chili, Bubba's 35
Cream of Artichoke Soup, Court
Street Cafe 51
Curry-Crab Soup, Tally-Ho
Restaurant 119
French Onion Soup, Cragsmere
Manna 23
French Onion Soup with Sherry
and Mushrooms, The Wash
House Restaurant 179
Ham and Corn Chowder,
Cragsmere Manna 179
Lemon Chicken Orzo Soup,
Sweetbriar Restaurant 24
Red Beans and Rice Soup, Major
Grumbles 116
Tuscan Tomato and Bread Soup,
Arman's at ParkLane 71
Uncle Bud's Seafood Gumbo, The
Grand Dining Room 175

Vegetables and Side Dishes
Asparagus Casserole, Hotel Talisi
Restaurant 151
Butterbean Cakes, Justine's
Courtyard & Carriageway 191
Cornbread Dressing, Sassafras Tea
Room 147
Crawfish-Andouille Grits, Mezza-
nine 104
Cuban Black Beans, Behind the
Glass 155
Fennel Mashed Potatoes, The
Victoria 4
Fried Green Tomatoes, The
Irondale Cafe 83
Garlic Mashed Potatoes, The
Silvertron Cafe 92
Heavenly Carrots, Garland
House 163
Saffron-Lobster Risotto, Mezza-
nine 104
Spanakopita, Nabeel's Cafe 88
Spinach and Rice Casserole, The
Bright Star 95
Squash Casserole, The Olde
Warehouse 7
Squash Dressing, Red's Little
School House 135
Sweet Potato Soufflé, Sassafras Tea
Room 147
Tomato Pie, The Gift Horse 171
Twice-Cooked Potato Casserole,
Bubba's 35
Twice-Baked Potatoes, Arman's at
ParkLane 72